Red Furrell
Box 25
Okahumpka Fl, 34762
352-406-4884

Tall sawgrass

James Carlton Fussell

Published 2016
Barefoot Publications
Okahumpka, Florida

This book is a work of truth and fiction. Several names are the product of the author's imagination. The location and several characters are their actual names. The book was written to preserve the history of Okahumpka and the lives of how the poorest of poor lived.

Transcribed and edited by Sandy Oard Kruse
Editing and book design by Ruth McIntyre Williams

Photo Credits

Cover-Bugg Spring — Sandy Oard Kruse

Title Page-Sawgrass — Open Stock

Okahumpka Map xii — Kay A. Eaton

Red and Byron xiv
  Red — Ruth McIntyre Williams
  Byron — Sandy Oard Kruse

Red at Ten xvi — Red Fussell Collection

White School 7 — Red Fussell Collection

A Big Snake 18 — Red Fussell Collection

Red and Byron 31 — Red Fussell Collection

Rosewall School 48 — Sandy Oard Kruse

Tennis Shoe 53 — Open Stock

Rabbit Tobacco 57 — Open Stock

Red with Bass 104 — Red Fussell Collection

Kaolin Mine 115 — Red Fussell Collection

Okahumpka Chapel 171 — Red Fussell Collection

Red at Fifteen or Sixteen 224 — Red Fussell Collection

Cat-eye Biskits 225 — Open Stock

List of Tales

Okahumpka in Red's Boyhood Days

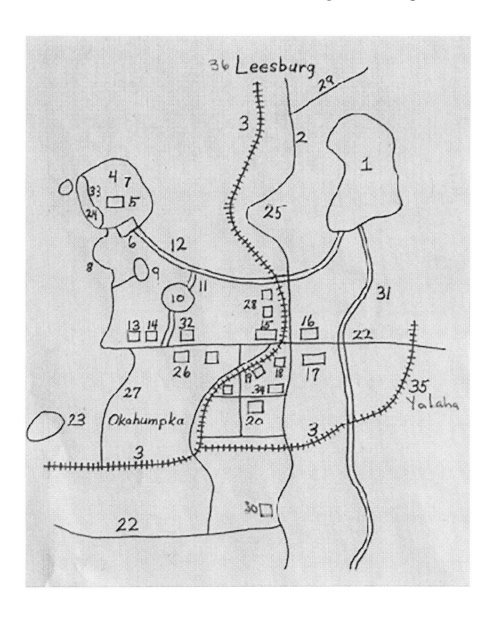

Locations on Map

1. Lake Harris
2. Highway 27 (current Hwy 33)
3. Atlantic Coast Line Railroad
4. Lake Denham
5. Island
6. Cason Swamp
7. Spring
8. Stage Coach Rd
9. Uncle Will's House
10. Bugg Spring
11. Bugg Spring Run
12. Helena Run
13. Byron's House
14. Two-Story House
15. Beer Joint
16. Tex's Store
17. Bowling Alley
18. Mr. Hall's Store
19. Depot
20. Red's House
21. Hwy 470 – Dirt Rd, then Clayed
22. Hwy 48
23. Wallet Pond
24. The Log We Walked On
25. Sawgrass Curve
26. Hotel with 100 Rooms
27. Bay Street
28. Quarters
29. Dixie Ave
30. Club 48
31. Creek
32. Post Office
33. Denham Swamp
34. School House
35. Yalaha
36. Leesburg
37. Baptist Church
38. Rosewood School for the black children

The boys today,
now in their 80's.

Red

Byron

Preface

This book is titled *Tall Sawgrass*. If you've ever been in sawgrass, you know that it has very sharp edges, and it will cut you from head to toe and tear your clothes.

The story is 'bout two young boys growin' up in Okahumpka, Florida. Carlton, that's me; but I was always called Red—still am today. Byron was my best friend. The story is 'bout poverty, love and two boys 'bout 8 and 9 years old. Byron and I are in our 80's today and we are still best friends. He and I both put many of our stories in this book.

We had an ole colored gentleman somewhere around 85-89 years old as a friend. We called 'im Uncle Will. He didn't know when he was born or where he was born, and we really loved 'im.

Uncle Will lived over on the edge of the Bugg Spring Swamp. The swamp ran a purty good ways, probably 7 to 8 miles and had lots of mud, snakes and gators. It had coons and possums, and two young boys and Uncle Will. Will lived in a little log cabin. There warn't no runnin' water in it; there were an outside privy and a pitcher pump outside.

He had one big ole pot and a woodstove inside, no 'frigerator. There warn't no washin' machine and he didn't take a bath too often. He smelled bad sometimes, but that was alright 'cause it didn't make no difference to us whether he took a bath or not. Now, he did have a factory-made corncob pipe and every once in a while he'd let us have a drag on it.

Some of this book is true, and some of it's not. I'll let you decide what you want to believe and what you don't. I hope you enjoy readin' it. I enjoyed doin' it. I loved the friendship that I had with these people and wouldn't trade it for a different life growin' up.

Red

Red at ten

The Swamp

Chapter 1

Back in 'bout 1940, when I was 8 or 9, I run into the house and told my mama, "In 15 minutes I'm gonna go over to the swamp."

And she would always tell me the same thang, "Don't get snake-bit." Like I was goin' to go over there and wrestle me up a rattlesnake and let 'im bite me.

So I grabbed my .22 and my box of .22 bullets and I went by Byron's house and I said, "Wanna go to the swamp?"

And he said, "Yup!"

He grabbed his .45-70 and we went into the swamp. His shells had done turned yellow and green, but I wanna tell you what kind of shot he were. When he cracked down on it, it's dead!!

So we built us a platform over there in Bugg Spring, which lays off of Bugg Spring Run and we'd built it up 'bout 20 feet off the ground. We built it with whatever scraps we could find; if we could find a scrap that would work good, we'd use that thang in there and put it up. So we took and built this platform from some used screen and some used tin and we put it up there. And Uncle Will, he told us how to make a mattress. You take an ole feed sack, whatever you want to call 'em, and you cut this real tall grass, and you put it inside there and it made it nice and soft. Takes a long time to cut that grass 'cause it piles up inside jist a little bit.

So when I first made that bed it had a tin roof over it, which was real rusty-lookin' tin, and it was 'bout 3 foot high. So really, whenever we got there we layed down.We'd go up there and lay on top of this in the treetops and the wind would blow and it'd crack and it'd rumble and it made all kinds of noises. All the squirrels would come by and the snakes, but no gators.

Lake Denham's swamp's a bad swamp. You could get lost in that thang on a good day. And we'd been all over it. We had trails everywhere. But whenever you went into this island it had mist. The big cypress on this island and the big pine trees probably took up to 3 acres. And the gators was in there. And the hogs. And all these other thangs that we liked.

So we was gonna go in there and we hauled in them boards and built us another platform up there 'bout 15 to 20 feet. When you get in that high 'em skeeters don't eat you up so bad. But there's a plant, I don't know what the name of it is, but we'd rub that plant on us, and that'd keep some of the skeeters off. But they was so bad down there that whenever you'd breathe you'd be sucking 'em up your nose. So we'd get up in the treetops and the skeeters warn't so bad.

We built that platform and we had us a ladder nailed onto the tree and a place we climbed up through. We decided that we'd go over there and spend the day. And then we'd kill hogs. We needed a hog hide. We got us some of 'em cyprus logs that the center had rotted out of, and we took a hew ax and went inside and hewed that thang so it was much thinner than it was. And then we'd stretch our hog skin over the end of that log and put a hole in the middle of it. Then we'd drag a resin ball across it and it would make a really scary sound. That way we could be over there at nighttime and if anyone come out there they'd think it were boogers in that swamp, and they'd stay away from us.

We climbed up on our platform, sat on it and looked down and there was a great big gator 'bout twenty feet away from us. He'd been waitin' for a meal too. We didn't bother 'im 'cause we didn't want to kill 'Ole Joe; we'd known 'im for a few years. He'd been in there and everyone talked 'bout how big he was and how bad he was. So, Ole Joe layed there and we looked up and here come a coon walkin' the edge of the thang. Ole Joe swum to it; jist set down and watched 'im, that coon. That coon would go out there and run 'round the water, and then he made the mistake of walkin' in front of 'Ole Joe. Joe grabbed 'im, twisted 'im and he squealed and 'Ole Joe swallowed 'im. I told Byron, I said, "He's still not done squealin'."

He said, "Nope, he ain't," he said, "but if he'd done swallowed you, I woulda cut his belly and got you out."

So then we looked at 'im and he left for a couple of hours and we watched all them varmints. Then we got down and walked the cyprus log back out. If you don't walk on the log out, the mud is 'bout waist deep to a big man, and we warn't very big. So we always made sure we walked it out and didn't leave no trail 'cause we was barefooted. We was always barefoot and only put our shoes on if we had to go to school or church.

We went all the way back to Cason Hammock, climbed up in there and layed there for a while. Got our corncob pipes out; them warn't factory built, them were homemade. Uncle Will made 'em for us. And we got our rabbit tobacco out that we'd cut up in little itty-bitty pieces and we put pinches in our pipes, sat down and smoked our pipes. Had to strike more matches and light that thang up, and we'd sit there and watch the varmints go by. Then all of a sudden we hear this awful squawk, "Raarr! Raaarr," it said.

"What's that?" says Byron.

And I said, "I don't know!"

We looked all round the ground and we couldn't see nothin'. We heared diggin' and he said, "It's the boogers!" We eased over to an edge where we could look out. We looked up and there was a bobcat there. Somehow that thang had climbed up the tree while we was gone and then we climbed up it and he's up and we's up it!!

I tell Byron, "You wanna shoot it?"

"Don't shoot it! We ain't gonna eat 'im and we ain't gonna skin 'im. If we ain't gonna do that, let 'im be." Said, "As soon as we leave, he'll leave."

So it be gettin' a little late in the afternoon, 'bout 3:30—4 o'clock. We decided that we'd go home. We go down and went around behind by Uncle Will's. He was sittin' down outside in an ole chair that shoulda been burned a long time ago. He said, "You boys see anythin' out there?"

I tell 'im, "Oh, we saw a wildcat and an ole hog."

And he said, "I wanna tell y'all somethin'. They's a big snake in that thang. That thang is 30-foot long."

I said, "Uncle Will, you sure 'bout that?"

He said, "Yeah, I'm sure. I didn't see it, but Mr. Georgeson, he's a snake catcher and he's scared to mess with it. I think you boys better stay out of that-there swamp."

I said, "Uncle Will, we ain't gonna stay out of that swamp." Said, "Why don't Mr. Georgeson catch it?"

He said, "It's a rattlesnake."

I said, "Ooh!"

"It's got fangs on it look like a 16-penny nail."

"Whew Doggie, must be big!"

He said, "Its head can hardly fit in a water bucket."

Said, "NO! Uncle Will."

"How come? You boys ask Mr. Georgeson. Mr. Georgeson is a snake hunter; he does that for a livin' and he's scared of it, and y'all jist little ole kids." And he said, "You need to stay out of that-there swamp."

"We can't stay out of that swamp. That's the only place we got."

"Y'all jist young 'uns. You got no business in there. I have a mind to go tell yer mama what y'all doin'. She would skin your behinds!"

"No, don't do that!"

So we left Uncle Will and went back out across the pond behind Byron's house. Went down by the cow pen. We got to swingin' on the swing and we put our guns up next to the tree and hopped on the swing. The swing was an old feed sack full of moss wrapped up. The stuff to hang the swing with, well, the army had a surplus over in the woods back there and they had telephone line. We jist cut off a section big enough. We cut off 10 sections and then we'd tie an entire thang to a tree and plait that thang out like you would a whip. And then we had it all hangin' down there in the cow pen. And every day, everybody would gather round and we'd swing.

No one ever knowed what we was doin' in the swamp. So we'd go there and sleep sometimes. We'd swing over the pond and then it'd swing back and another one would jump on and another one would jump on and the next thang you knowed, 5 or 6 of us would be swingin' on that one ole swing. It was fun!

So I said, "I've gotta get on home; it's gettin' dark." And I said, "Yep, Monday I'm a-goin' to school."

Byron said, "Ok."

So I grabbed my .22 and my .22 bullets and headed across the pasture. I got home and my mama wanted to know if I'd seen anythin' over there. And I said, "Yeah, we seen an ole hog and bobcat and a couple of coons, nothin' real important."

She said, "Ok. Well, it's time for your Saturday bath." And I was stinky. I didn't like to take that bath. Our ole washtub, you pumped the water into it. I warn't the first one that got the bath. My momma got it first, my daddy got it second, my brother got it third and I got it last. So my brother pumped the water; everyone used the same water. But it was gettin' close to the winter time, so it was purty cold. And they'd put it over by the fireplace. Whenever you'd take your bath, that one side of the tub would be a little closer to the fire. And that thang burned a streak on your behind. And it was only Saturday baths, not Monday, not Tuesday, not Wednesday, not Thursday, not Friday. It was Saturday when you took your bath. You washed your feet, you washed your face, you washed your hands and then you went to bed on 'em other days.

The School

Chapter 2

The kind of school we went to was a big ole buildin' with rooms there. The auditorium—it held 200 people. They was jist 5 classes, all in one classroom, first through the fifth. Now we was in the third grade 'bout this time. We had a good teacher and we loved her to death. She was a beautiful woman and she's still that today. Well, they had a lunchroom. Cost a nickel to eat in the lunchroom. But my dad give 'em sweet taters and beans and peas and okra and all that stuff that he grew. We didn't have the nickel but I could eat in the lunchroom free.

The teacher couldn't spell, so none of us learnt how to spell, 'cept Byron. I don't know how he learnt how to spell. He always said that they wanted 'im to come to school so that they could keep the school runnin'. But I always believed that his mama wanted 'im out of the house.

We had but one girl in our class. Her name was Evelyn. Evelyn could scrap a boy! You cross her and she'd tear your shirt off and throw you down in the dirt and rub your nose in that clay out in the front. So, one day she ate Byron's apple and the teacher whipped her for it. But that don't settle nothin'. We gonna settle the rest of this at the depot!

We went down to the depot after school was out and Byron got a lucky punch in and blacked her eye. And she left and went on home and the next mornin' she come to school with that black eye. The teacher wanted to know who did it and we said, "Byron done it!"

"Well," she said. "Hmm. Somebody go get me a switch." He was my friend so I went and got one. I went off to the plum trees. I wanted to get a good one 'cause I wanted to hear 'im holler. She put a whippin' on 'im! I'd call it a beatin'! She whipped 'im and told 'im if he ever hit another girl she would really put a beatin' on 'im, with all the muscle she got! She put stripes on his behind and on his legs.

We was walkin' down the clay road goin' home and they was tears in his eyes. He said, "I don't think I can stand no more."

The school was jist off the highway, right off 33. Now there warn't no runnin' water in this school. The pump burned up and they never replaced it. So what we did was, the older boys would go out there in the field and they'd get a bucket of water for the boy's bathroom and a bucket of water for the girl's bathroom.

Finally, they closed the school down; we jist didn't have enough kids to go there. We went to sixth grade and then we went to the "big school" when the leaves turned.

We went to the "big school" and they kind of burned us down a little bit; they called us white trash" and they was probably right. We was comin' in there, and we didn't wear no shoes in the country school. I had a pair of tennis shoes I wore to high school—the "big school", I called it. But the big boys beat on the small ones.

White school

Fishin', Bill, and the Snake

Chapter 3

We'd fish quite a bit. We'd fish the ponds and then we'd go take our catch to Will and he'd cook 'em and we'd eat 'em. And he put plenty of salt on it. He'd cook out in the fry pan; we'd eat out of the ole pot. We had our own forks. We had to hang it on our own nail in Will's cabin and we washed it sometimes, but not often.

Well, a man gave us an ole boat and the thang weighed a ton. I tried to get my daddy to take it down to Wallet Pond, but he said, "Nope." We couldn't get no one to take it to Wallet Pond. So what we did was, we decided we'd push it down the railroad track. So we nailed some tin on the bottom of this boat and we started pushin'. And we pushed that thang and the minute we got it down to where the stream is we heared the train comin'!! So we got it off the track and started to run. The train went by and they looked at us real funny. We pulled it right back on the track and we started pushin' again. We pushed it all day long. We pushed that boat a mile and a half, maybe two miles down that track. We got down there and we took it across the track and got it up by the bank.

And finally we got it to Wallet Pond. The next day we went down to go fishin' in our new boat but all the sides had leaked. They'd swelled up and they all leaked. We stuffed thangs in the cracks and they'd still leak. You had to have your coffee tin to dip the water out so it didn't sink.

So we fished, and we caught some fish. We pulled 'em out on the bank and cleaned 'em up, went down the railroad tracks and cut 'em up. Went to Uncle Will's house and took 'em fish in there and we cooked 'em up and went out on the porch and enjoyed 'em.

I said, "It's Thursday so I gotta get home. Friday I gotta cut my wood so I can go to the swamp. I've gotta milk the cow."

Saturday mornin' we decided to go again and fish. So we take off down the railroad tracks. We got down there and take out the boat and here come Bill. He's ridin' around in an ole truck and he says, "Boys, bring my boat to the bank."

It warn't his boat, but we was scared of 'im 'cause he was probably 22 or 23 years older and here we was jist ten years old. We knowed if we didn't bring it to the bank, he'd take his gun out. So we brought it to the bank and watched 'im paddle off in that boat. So we went back home, went down to the depot and got our corncob pipes out and took out our rabbit tobacco. And sittin' at the depot, we watched the train go by. Then we finally figured out that we was gonna get even Monday after-noon when we got out of school.

We went down to Wallet Pond and drilled a hole in our boat. We put a cork in it, a rusty ole dirty-lookin' cork. Then we saw Bill go by in his truck and I thought, *We got 'im now!*

So we took off down the railroad track and they was a gully and a clay pit this side of Wallet Pond so it took us a while, but we got there before too long. Bill was paddlin' out there in our boat but nothin' had happened. Then he got to movin' around and that cork done come out and that ole boat sunk to the bottom. It sunk and he had his shoes on and his jacket on. He got to the bank but all of his fishin' tackle was buried down there in the bottom of Wallet Pond.

We knowed that if'n he caught us, we was in bad trouble. So we left and we went down the railroad tracks. We didn't walk in the sand in the road, 'cause we didn't want anyone to see where we had been. And we'd go through the field to keep 'im from knowin' what we was doin' over there. We went by Byron's house and he got his rifle.

We went down to the swamp and we was layin' up there in the trees and we heared a noise comin' toward us through the woods. We'd trained ourselves to know all the noises we would hear. Said, "That's that snake."

So Byron turns around with his rifle, gets all ready, and I could jist see that hundred dollars already we'd get for the skin. But you know what? Here come Bill! He come up where we had that hog skin over that log and takes his knife out and bends over and his hat fell off. He put it back on and bent over and it fell off again. And then he set it up on top of that log.

Well, he took his knife out and cut that skin on that log that we had. And we set there and watched it. I said, "Byron, shoot his hat." Now Byron, he was good at that rifle. Bill bent down to cut the rest of the hide off that log, and "Bam!!" That log jumped and that wood splintered and "Bam!!" He shot that log again. He put another round in and Bill run down 'bout 30 feet to get into the trail that went by the platform and I said, "Shoot that limb" and Byron shot the limb jist in front of 'im and the limb fell. Whenever it fell he run out there by the meadows.

That meadow's got sawgrass on it too. He run up through 'em meadows and had his arms up. When he run back through that trail, "Bam!!" The limb fell right in the middle of it, so he run out there hollerin' and screamin'. Well, we scared 'im. He knowed it was us but he didn't know where we was at. He didn't look up in that tree so we stayed up there probably an hour or two and then we heared that noise again.

Said, "Oh, here comes that snake or here comes Bill with a gun and he'll shoot us out of the tree."

But we seen Uncle Will and he says, "Hey, boys." He didn't know we had that place; it was camouflaged with moss purty good.

"Hey, Uncle Will."

He said, "What y'all boys shootin' at?"

"We shootin' at Bill."

Shakin' his head he says, "Boys, what are y'all gonna do next?"

I said, "Well, he took our boat and then he come down here and cut our hog skin up."

He said, "Y'all gonna be in jail afore you know it."

"We ain't gonna be in jail." Said, "We gonna bring a chicken down tomorrow and you can cook it."

He said, "Alright, I'll cook it for you." He went down there and looked where we shot that limb off the first tree. He looked at the second one. "Crack shot. He good." He went up there and picked ole Bill's hat up. And it was all up in pieces. I mean it was tore up!

We went down to the store. Gonna get us a can of Prince Albert and we see Bill. I thought, *We're a goner. He don't know who done it, but he knowed who was down there.*

He said, "I'm gonna tell you boys somethin'."

We said, "Bill, you stole our boat, then you sunk our boat. How'd you do that?"

I said, "I'm gonna tell my daddy on you and see what he does."

And then he said, "Why don't we jist forget it?"

I said, "Ok, we'll forget it."

Well, we really wanted a boat! Uncle Will had what used to be a boat out by his cabin but it had a few holes in it. So what we done was we went out there and pulled it to where we could work on it a bit. We found some pieces of wood and some ole rags to put in the holes and Uncle Will had some black sticky stuff in a can out there. We had no idea what it was but boy, was it sticky!! So we slapped that sticky stuff on the boat and purty much glued the rags and the patches to the boat. We pulled the boat down by the water so's it could dry real good.

Then we couldn't get that-there sticky stuff off our hands. Said, "My mama's a-gonna get real mad at me with all this sticky stuff on my hands." And she was. It jist had to wear off our hands.

So the next afternoon we went down to the Wallet Pond to take out our boat and go fishin'. Guess what? The boat was gone! I don't know whether Bill stole it, or what, but it was gone.

'Bout a year later, that boat wound up in Lake Denham. So we knowed somebody had got to it. So we brung a large mule, hitched it to the boat and drug that thang down Bay Street, turned down by the railroad tracks, went through there. Whenever we got down to Wallet Pond, we had to cross them rocks so much we wore the bottom down. That's the thang we was afraid of. So we put it down over on the pile and put it on fire and burned it up.

Saturday mornin', I woke up bright and early, got my .22 and Byron got his rifle and I said, "You know we told Uncle Will that we was gonna get 'im a chicken to cook. We can still get one of 'em. You like that?"

He said, "Yeah, that's alright." So we'll jist go get this chicken and he said, "You think Uncle Will will miss a chicken?" So we reached in his pen there and grabbed us a chicken, wrung his neck and plucked the feathers off 'im to fry 'im up. He warn't big, but boy, he was good. Will always salted everythin' really good.

We only had one cup. We all drank outta the same cup. So we got all our food and ate up all our chicken and then we headed down toward the swamp.

We went over there on the Lake Denham side of the swamp to see if we could see that rattlesnake. So we climbed up on the boards and layed down up there until we heared a noise comin' through the saw-grass. I mean, it was movin'! And then a gator come out. So what that gator do is he had the sunshine over to 'bout jist his feet.

And I asked Byron what he was doin'. And Byron says, "You know I coulda killed 'im." Said, "Jist gimme a second."

And I said, "No, that won't do."

Well, we layed up there probably for a couple of hours and then we decided we should get goin' right across that swamp. "Bet I coulda killed it," said Byron. But he couldn't kill it if his rifle was hangin' right down by his side.

I said, "It's huge. The thang probably would be two-foot thick. And he was movin', I'm a-tellin' ya."

And whenever that snake come around, everythin' in that swamp went still. Lots of noise in that thang. So we layed up there hopin' that snake would come back 'cause this time we was ready for it. And we looked over to the end of the island. The west part runs into everythin'. And we knowed we couldn't get over there and back, which was too dangerous a thang to do. So, as life would have it, we missed our snake.

We was layin' up there and we watched a hog go by, they was 'bout four little pigs. We thought 'bout killin' one of the pigs, then said, "Nah, let 'em grow up. Let 'em run up against a gator and he'll have 'em for lunch."

So, then we hear the gator goin' after the hog; hog's a good swimmer. Then nighttime was comin' on so we climbed down. I said, "Byron, we can go to Uncle Will's or we can sleep up in the tree."

He said, "Nah, let's go to Uncle Will's."

So we went down there to Uncle Will's. He had a board hangin' on a nail on the side of the ole log house he lived in. That's what he slept on and then he had two more boards nailed on the side for us. When we got there he was scared to death.

We said, "Uncle Will, what happened?"

He said, "That snake come down here and he looked in at me."

I said, "How you know he looked in on you?

He said, "I was standin' at the window. I looked through that shutter and I seen his eyeball, and he scared me to death."

And then he said, "Did you boys steal my chicken?"

We said, "No, we didn't steal your chicken."

He said, "Well, I got one chicken missin' and that chicken we ate was a fine cooked chicken."

So I said, "Yeah, we took it."

He said, "I was plannin' on havin' that chicken for Christmas dinner! It was a big ole fat chicken. It was good; it was a good ole chicken."

So we said, "Ok, we'll get you 'nother chicken."

Then he said, "Boys, y'all better give that chicken back." So we knowed he was serious. He said, "It ain't no joke; y'all better get me a chicken. I can't get no chicken myself; they'll shoot a black man like me if I ever stole a chicken." Said, "What was you young'uns thinkin' 'bout?"

We said, "Don't worry 'bout it; we'll get you your chicken back." He didn't know that I got two chickens from the house that my mother told me to get. And we'd get eggs at the house and go down there and give 'em to 'im.

They was a fella named Joe who raised chickens. Will and Joe didn't get along too well together. Joe liked 'im, but Will didn't think Joe liked 'im. Whenever Joe saw 'im he asked 'im, "Did you get my two chickens?" and we always thought it was funny. Will would get so mad 'bout it. He jist didn't want us boys stealin' people's chickens.

He said, "Lord a-mercy, boys. Y'all gonna wind up in jail and get me shot."

So I said, "Well, we won't do that."

But he said "Y'all better stay outta 'em woods." He said, "Yeah, y'all better be careful down there in 'em woods. They's everythin' in there. They's moccasins and gators, everythin' down there is bad news. They's poison ivy."

We said, "Well, poison ivy don't bother us."

Here it is Friday again. We're back at the hammock down there and we gonna spend the night. We went down and dug us some stingin' nettle root and we dug up the thang that looked like a potato down there to make us some flour with. Had some rice and a little bit of corn meal and we took us fishin' poles and a hook. We took it down there and jiggled it in front of 'em frogs. And that frog'd grab that thang and we'd pop his butt off and skin his legs out. We looked in the water and saw one of 'em big ole soft shell turtles. Byron said, "You know what? I'd clean that soft shell turtle."

I said, "Ok." So we went down and got us some wire off that bale of hay down there in the barn and made us a loop and put a hand loop on it and borrowed someone's boat from down in Bugg Spring. We used it all the time down that way.

We was easin' down through there and Byron said, "Whew Doggie, look at that one!" And he got that wire and put a loop around its head and snuck up on it. I warn't sure who was gonna win. But he pulled the turtle's head up over the side and said, "Cut his throat." So I cut his throat. Turned the water red all over.

And I said, "Byron, we got trouble." I said, "They's mudfish everywhere you look." I guess they smelled that blood. We had a few snakes hangin' 'round there too. So we eased outta that thang, took that little snapping turtle and hung 'im on the side of the boat to cut his head off.

Took the turtle down to Uncle Will's and opened the shell off, got the legs and the neck and got the steak part of the turtle. He put it in a pot and said, "You gotta boil it for 'bout two hours."

So we said, "We'll be back."

We took off back down to the swamp and got our frog legs. We had 'bout ten, but somethin' didn't seem right. Jist had a feelin'. Somethin' jist warn't right. So we climbed up the tree and we sat there and said, "It's the snake." So Byron looked one way and I looked the other way. He loaded his .45-70.

He said, "Oh my! Look at 'im! They come a rattlesnake through the woods 'bout five feet long." He said, "I'm gonna nail his head to the ground." And he did. "POW!" and his head jist blew off. The snake was still tryin' to strike everythin' it could. It was strikin' even though its head was gone. It was strikin' at the trees and anythin' in its way.

I told 'im, I said, "That's somethin' else! He not gonna die 'til the sun goes down!"

The Snake Again, the Dogs and Georgeson

Chapter 4

He said, "I feel it too, but I don't see nothin' up here and they ain't nothin' back here." Said, "They's somethin' here; maybe it's that big, old snake. I mean to tell you that old hog run out and it was squealin'. Grabbed that rattlesnake and run off with it."

And I thought, *What in the world*! I mean he was huge. You could hear 'im rubbin' 'em teeth inside that thang. We stayed up a couple more hours after this; after we seen the hog and the snake and everythin' quieted down around the swamp. It jist got dark so we decided we'd better go to Uncle Will's and see if he cooked that turtle good. So we climbed off and got on the trail and went by his house. We got there and he didn't look quite right.

We said, "What's wrong, Will?"

He said, "That ole snake come by here again."

I said, "Why didn't you show 'im that rifle you got?"

He said, "Lordy, boy! If you miss that thang he'll eat you up alive. That thang is huge!" He showed us where he saw it. It left a big track.

I asked, "Well, you got the turtle cooked"?

He said, "Yeah, I got the turtle cooked." He said, "I cooked up some cabbage in there; it'd better be good."

So we all got in there and got us a turtle leg and we et that meat off the leg. It was a big pile of meat. And et us some potatoes and carrots and got jist 'bout everythin' you can think of that was way down at the bottom of the pot.

Will said, "You boys goin' back to the swamp?"

We said, "Naw, we're gonna go home. We had a long day today but we gonna come back tomorrow and kill that snake."

He said, "Y'all better leave that thang alone. That thang's dangerous."

Said, "Well, we got to do somethin' with 'im since he's worth a hundred dollars dead and we ain't never had a hundred dollars."

He said, "Yeah, but if he kills you, that hundred dollars ain't no good."

Said, "We ain't gonna let 'im kill us. We got a dog. He ain't gonna let that snake kill us."

He said, "I bet he kills yer dog."

We said, "Naw, that dog's smart."

So we went on home and the next mornin' we got up bright and early and I went to Byron's house. He had to take and pump the water for his mama to wash with, so I helped 'im pump the water. We pumped the water and got a tub full and went outside and it looked like it might rain a little bit. So we took off now and said we'd come back by supper time.

So we left and went down and kept seein' dog tracks down there. We never thought much 'bout it so we climbed up to our platform on Lake Denham side and we heared it comin' through the woods. We didn't see 'im anywhere. And then we saw 'bout ten or twelve dogs. You could tell who the leader was. It was a little cur, and he was a good 50 yards behind us, this little cur dog.

And Byron said, "Good as done." POW! and guess what. He fell to the ground. Them other dogs couldn't tell where that shot come from 'cause it was above 'em. They ran every which way. Three of 'em ran down by that bank. And right on the edge of that water was gators. The gator caught the one, and on the other side over there was three more gators and they got two more of 'em dogs there.

But they was still three underneath the tree. I didn't want to shoot 'em under the tree. I said, "I'm gonna shoot that one in the foot. And whenever he runs off, you kill it." They was vicious dogs. They'd been killin' cows. And the men who owned the cows told us if we saw any dogs, to shoot 'em. They made a pass to run up there and whenever he made that pass on the left-hand side that's when the gator caught 'im.

We thought, *We only got two left.*

He said, "Shoot the tail off the little dog there and I'll take care of it." Whenever I shot the tail off the dog, he made a run and he was there and out; but Byron had an ole .45-70, so he busted 'im on the right. We had one dog left and he was under the tree, and he warn't really happy. He didn't exactly know where he was goin'. But he knowed he didn't want to leave under there 'cause that seemed to be the safest place.

And then we heared this noise comin'. We said, "There comes our snake. We gonna get that snake." And lo and behold, you won't never guess what walked out—Georgeson, the snake man. He'd been after that big ole rattlesnake off and on, on that island to the right of us. And he had one in a sack. We said, "George, this dog here is bad underneath this tree."

He said, "Yeah, I know 'em dogs. They killed all my chickens the other night." He said, "Shoot the dog and I'll throw 'im to the gator."

We said, "Ok." Took my .22 to a crack in the floor and "BAM!" The dog fell. Georgeson walked up there and hung his sack on the side of the ladder and picked the dog up and threw it over there. That gator done got supper twice that day. He grabbed 'im up and then another gator come up and they fought over 'im.

We looked at 'em. They was over there tearin' that dog all to pieces. So we climbed down off that tree and Georgeson, the snake man, was standin' there and said that he had a purty nice rattlesnake in the sack.

I said, "Ain't you 'fraid to carry 'imt around in a sack?"

He said, "Oh, no, it don't bite through the sack."

I said, "Hmm, you know, I still ain't carryin' none in no sack."

So then we started to head out and Georgeson said, "Where y'all goin'?"

We said, "Georgeson, there's a log here that you can walk in and walk out on."

He said, "I never knowed that."

I said, "Let me show you." Said, "We don't leave no trail 'cause we don't want nobody in here 'cept us."

He said, "Well, I knowed 'bout the island but I don't say nothin' 'bout it. It ain't no big deal."

So then we waded on through and he said, "You got all 'em dogs taken care of? They all gone?"

Said, " Them gators have done et 'em up."

He said, "They bad dogs. They kill every one of my chickens. They kill 'em for the fun of it."

I said, "Well, they won't kill 'em no more."

He said, "How y'all gonna kill that snake?

Said "We gonna shoot the head off'n 'im."

He said, "If it was me I'd snare 'im. I'd snare that snake."

We said, "That's what we was goin' after." Said, "Uncle Will seen 'im twice. He been by his house."

He said, "He been by my house too. He's a night crawler. He's tryin' to get everybody scared to go out at nighttime 'cause you don't know when he's gonna come by and catch you."

I said, "Well, we're fixin' to go home; it's gettin' dark. Tomorrow mornin' I can't come back 'cause it's washday and my brother's workin', so I gotta get the water. But we gonna come back here and we gonna get that snake."

We left Georgeson up on the end of the grove and we headed back down to where Stagecoach Road was. And we went across that. We looked and guess what we saw? That big ole snake had crossed that gully and he was headed towards Cason Hammock.

We said, "We went the wrong direction today. I bet he went right by that!"

A big snake, but not the one Red and Byron chased.

Other Goin's-On in the Swamp

Chapter 5

Well, I decided to bring my old cur dog and see what I could do with it on Monday or Tuesday. I got to thinkin' 'bout it and said, "You know what, if he go out there and chases that snake, I ain't much wantin' to go into that marsh." But I'd do it that way anyway.

So Tuesday I got my .22 and my bullets and I went down by Byron's. Byron was sittin' out front waitin' for me. He had his .45-70 and 'bout a dozen shells. We went down by the mud and walked up the hill where Uncle Will was at.

And Uncle Will said, "You know somethin' boys?" Said, "They makin' shine up in them woods. But they don't set up the colored folk like me."

I said, "How do you know"?

He said, "Look, one of 'em food jars is 25 cents."

I said, "I've got 25 cents. Me and Byron killed a gator and skinned it out. We got 'bout 10 dollars apiece for it. I kept 2 dollars of it and gave my mama the rest of it. So I had a quarter.

We took that afternoon and went down across the creek to take the cable hand over hand. We got to the other side and we got down and went over there in that swamp. They was a hole out there in the swamp and a little ole man. He had 'bout 4 fruit jars sittin' over there, and a cup. So we put a quarter in and got us a fruit jar. We carried it back down with our rifles and eased back down through there and thought maybe we'd see a snake or somethin'. Got all the way up to Uncle Will's house and told Uncle Will, "We got you some water." We give 'im that and he shook it and said, "Lord-a-mercy, boys. Swamp water. Where y'all get this?"

We said, "That ole Bastille."

He said, "That man, he got you with this. He'd kill an ole black man with this. What are you tryin' to do, get me killed?"

I said, "I didn't tell you to drink none of it."

He said, "I don't think I want no more of that."

So we et lunch with Uncle Will. We et the rest of that turtle up and it were gettin' a little bit sour but we ate it anyway. We eased on back down towards Lake Denham and there that snake had crossed again. He was goin' back towards Cason Hammock. So we decided we'd give Cason Hammock a run. We went out there and climbed up on our deck and got down our screen and layed down. They warn't much goin' on all day. It was quiet. Too quiet. We saw some movement in the brush. Out walks an ole sow. The poor pig walks across there and lays down in the hammock. There come a bobcat behind it and then this old snake.

I said, "Don't shoot that; that's a Blue Racer."

We layed there for 'bout another hour and then we heared the turkeys flyin' to the roost. He said, "I wanna kill a turkey."

I said, "I don't wanna clean it. There's lots of feathers to pick on a turkey." So we let the turkey go.

It was gettin' close to dark so we said, "Well, it's time to climb down again." We climbed out of that tree and stepped right on the biggest covy of quail you ever saw. But we thought sure we was standin' on a rattlesnake! And I thought that rattlesnake had done got me. I wanted to run, but I didn't.

We made us a quail trap out of ferns. We piled 'em up, plaited 'em together; then we put us a trap in there and we got us a couple handfuls of feed from Uncle Will. We told 'im we was gonna trap that quail, and he told us, "That game warden will put you into the jail for trappin' quail."

But when we brought 'em back to 'im, he walked back up to his house and cleaned the quail we caught. They was 'bout 4 in the trap.

We re-set the trap and each had a quail to take home to Will's and we ate 1 each. We fried 'em up in lard and it was good. I liked 'em.

As we was sittin' there, Byron said, "Somethin's wrong."

I said, "What's wrong?"

He said, "I don't know. But somethin's goin' on."

We looked up and that big snake went by Ole Will's house again. Byron grabbed his rifle and afore he could fire it had turned right and all you could see was the tail end of 'im. And Byron hollered at it, but it didn't stop; it sped up. And it headed to Cason Hammock, so we jumped up and ran up there. We run as hard as we could run down Stage Coach Road and turned to the right up there where the gate's at. We went down there and got up in our tree. We stayed there 'til it was almost dark. We got down and we heared the snake go through the woods. So we went back to Uncle Will's and said, "We're gonna go home and see what we can do."

So I went home and my mother wanted to know if I had supper and I said, "Yeah, I had supper. We had 'em quail we caught."

"Oh, you should have brought 'em home."

"Yeah, I'm sorry. I wanted to eat 'em."

The Spring and the Polecat

Chapter 6

The next mornin' I got up early, got my .22 and my bullets and told my mama I was over there in the woods. "If you could kill some squirrels," she said, "bring 'em home."

I said, "Ok."

So I went over to Byron's. He was asleep on the porch. He woke up and said, "Let's do somethin' different today. Let's go farther east next to where that spring is and them oak trees."

I said, "Ok. We can go over there." So, we went out down the Stage Coach Road and down towards Lake Denham and walked in the orange grove to see if they was any snake tracks. We saw 1 or 2 dog tracks. We went on back and shot us moccasins while we was goin' across. Went over to the spring, beautiful spring up under 'em live oak trees. We took off all our clothes and got in the spring. We soaked it up real good and washed up with the sand off the bottom of the spring. We decided we'd head north and thought maybe we could see that snake in there.

So we went on farther north and guess what? We found us somethin'. Really found somethin'! We found an ole sour polecat with two little ones. We decided we was gonna catch that polecat and de-musk it. Then we'd have us a polecat in the house that didn't stink. They say they make good pets. I don't know if they do or not, but they say they do. So we run up there and grab that polecat.

Well, it was more than I could handle. That thang sprayed me and it got Byron and we up-chucked. We up-chucked all over the place. I threw the polecat down. We went back to the spring and washed our clothes in the dirt. We rubbed 'em in the sand. We scrubbed ourselves. We did everythin'! But we still smelled like that polecat! So we said, "We'll go right up to Uncle Will's and see what he tells us."

We never knocked on his door. We jist walked in and he says, "Oh my!! Boys, what have you got into?"

We said, "Well, we got into a polecat."

He said, "Yeah, you did. You smell like one."

We said, "How do we get the smell off us?"

He said, "Warm milk'll take it off."

The only thought we had was to go to that cow a fellow milked every day and it was 'bout 4 o'clock in the afternoon. So we paddy-paddled up there with a bucket and we milked his cow for 'im.

So we went back to Uncle Will's and he said, "Lord a-mercy boys. Y'all done stole milk and brought it back down here. Pour me out a little bit so I can make some biskits with it. And y'all wash down with the rest of it." So we did.

We still smelled like a polecat. We didn't know what to do so I took my shirt and I threw it away. I knowed my mama would kill me for it but I threw it away. And when I threw mine away, Byron threw his away.

We walked to Byron's house and he took the rifle and set it down and his mama threatened 'im. She told 'im to go to the barn and that was where he would stay until he smelled better.

Well, I went home. I slept with my brother, but this time my brother said, "NO! you're not sleepin' in my bed." So they gave me a blanket and I went to the barn where the rats and the snakes was. I think they all left when I went in there!

To the Movies and Back

Chapter 7

Well, we went on down the next mornin'. I got up and I went to work pickin' potatoes. And we ate 'em little ole potatoes that they had 'til we got sick. And we worked the rest of the day and got seventy-five cents. He said they ain't gonna need us tomorrow, so we didn't show up the next day. We didn't know exactly what to do so we said, "Let's go to the movies."

So that's what we did. We hopped the freight train and rode it to Leesburg. And we got off the train and we walked down to the Palace Theater. It was 9 cents to get in. We paid her 9 cents and I can still see the woman sniffin' her nose at us. She was smellin' that ole polecat.

We went into the theater and sat down next to 'em people in there. And for some reason 1 of 'em fellas turned around and said, "My gosh, it smells like a polecat in here." And there was a guy sittin' there so we turned around and pointed to 'im. He got up and moved. We had the area right in there all to ourselves.

We set there all the way through the movie. We got out of the movie and it was probably 'bout 4:30-5 o'clock. So we started home. We walked down Dixie Avenue to get to 27. We stuck up our thumbs and a man stopped to pick us up and he said, "Golly, you boys are gonna stink up my car." He said, "I'll tell you what I'm gonna do, I'm gonna open up the trunk and you boys can ride in the trunk."

We said, "That'd be fine. That'd be fine." So we got in his trunk and we rode. He let us out in Okahumpka and we thanked 'im and closed the trunk down.

We was standin' there and they was an oak tree in the middle of the road where a sign had been torn down. And this fella drove up in this big ole car and said, "Which 1 of you dumb kids can tell me how to get to Sumterville?"

So we said, "Well, as you go down across through there to the second curve, 'bout a mile down, the mud starts. The mud is 'bout a mile down through there, and there's logs in it and limbs in it and everythin' else." And we watched 'im take off down the road.

Well, we hung around there for a little while watchin' the cars go by and the people come by. At 'bout an hour and a half later he come back. He was muddy from 1 end to the other. He got out and said, "I've a mind to beat me a couple of kids."

So we ran up behind the beer joint back there through the woods. Climbed up the tree with no rifle. That was a mistake! We sat there in that tree and this big ole cat come by. It warn't no bobcat! I don't know what it was. I never seen nothin' that big in the woods afore. He eased right through the woods and went right on down through towards Lake Denham Swamp over there.

I told Byron, I said, "If I'd had my rifle I'd have shot it."

He said, "No you wouldn't 'cause I wouldn'a let you." He said, "If you ain't gonna eat it or skin it, you ain't gonna kill it."

I said, "I 'gree with that."

Ridin' Pine Trees and Raftin'

Chapter 8

We still had a little bit of smell to us so we went down to Uncle Will's and he was sittin' there smokin'. He lets us get a drag of it before we'd give it back to 'im. And he'd always say, "Lord a-mercy boys, if'n your mama knowed I'm doin' this she'd come here and shoot me with that shotgun!"

Well, she knowed how much we loved 'im and she wouldn't of done nothin'. And we knowed that. Well, I got up the next mornin' and I thought, *Well, what do I think I'll do?* It'd done come Saturday mornin' and my mother jist informed me that come Monday mornin' I started back at school.

I didn't want to go to school. We hadn't killed that big snake yet and I wanted to kill that big snake afore we got back to school. But I knowed I was gonna have to go, so I might as well make up my mind and jist go on. So I said, "I'm gonna go down to Byron's for a little bit. I got the yard raked and I got my wood cut."

So I took off over to Byron's and he said, "I don't wanna go to the swamp today."

So I said, "Well, let's go ride some pine trees."

Now if you ain't never rode a pine tree you don't know what you missin'. You climb in the top of that limber pine tree and get that thang to swayin' back and forth and it'll bend over and you can get back on the ground. Then you find you another one. You get up there and do the same thang all over again.

Byron's sister wanted to go with us. I didn't care. We was always doin' this ridin' pine trees. So she climbed up this pine tree and got it to swayin' back and forth and rode it to the ground jist like we did. Then she climbed up another one, got that thang goin' back and forth and it snapped off 'bout a third from the ground and plopped her on the ground.

Byron said, "I sure hope it didn't kill her."

She wobbles around there a few minutes; then she gets up and says she was alright.

We walked down to the creek and rinsed our feet off. They warn't dirty; we jist didn't have no shoes on for 'bout a week. But anyway we went down to the creek and said, "Well, we don't want to get our clothes wet." So we stripped off down to our underwear. If she hadn't have been there we'd have stripped off all of it; but she was there so we jist stripped to our underwear.

So we went down and we was sittin' in the water, knee-deep, watchin' the fish and whatever else, and we got to noticin' the grass on the bottom. Said, "Look at that grass on the bottom."

Byron reached down and got 'im a handful of it and broke it and it floated. He said, "You know we could make us a raft out of that!"

He was 'bout waist deep in there. We'd break ourselves off handfuls and hand 'em to Betty Jean; she was Byron's sister. She'd wrap 'em up good and tie it up with the grass and purty soon we had us a six-foot raft already made. We layed two layers of that grass on it and put the thang up front to put our chin on, and we was gonna raft down the creek. We got us two sticks to push it down the bank and hit the snakes if we saw some. And they was always plenty of snakes.

So we get in the creek and idle along as the day passed and it was warm and it felt good. We come on down 'bout halfway and we heared somebody talkin'. Well, we knowed better than to come up on some-body talkin' and not know who it was, 'cause that Mr. Bill, he'd probably drown us if he caught us. 'Specially if he knowed what we done to 'im. But we listened and they was jist laughin' and talkin' so we knowed it warn't 'im.

We eased down through there and come around this corner and

they was four black women down there. I don't know if they was takin' a bath or what, but they didn't have no clothes on. We rounded that bend. They stood up and gave us some choice words. And 1 of 'em was big! I mean BIG! So Byron and I said, "Boy! if she sat down on you, she'd crush you!"

Well, we went on down the creek; got down to the bridge and pulled the thang over to the side and climbed off. And of course, we was wet from 1 end to the other, so we walked home. We walked down the highway. It was a hogback road. The center is higher than the rest of it so the water runs off of it. So we walked down the road by the store. I went down the clay road towards the depot, and that 'bout ended that day.

I got home 'bout 5 o'clock. I already had my bath, that's what I told my mamma. I'd done took my bath in the creek. Well, she didn't go along with that too good and they done used the wash water to scrub the porch with, so she made me pump my own bath water.

She said, "Well, we'll have to heat up some more water."

I said, "Nah, I'll jist take a bath in that water." I didn't even want to take bath. I done got cleaned. The only thang dirty was my feet, but she insisted, so I took it. That was better than gittin' a whippin'.

Cane Grindin' to Make S'rup

Chapter 9

It was cool in September and the cane had to be cut but the tassels had to be cut off first. I asked Byron to help me. My dad made us two pieces of wood, sharp on 1 side. Friday afternoon we started to knock the tassels off. It was hard work. We had some of it done when help come, and I sure was glad to see the help. It were done in no time.

They started to cut the cane. But my dad didn't want Byron and me to cut cane. Said we might cut our foot off. It didn't take long to cut. They brung Henry's ole mule to pull the wagon. We filled the wagon with blue ribbon cane, that's the best stuff, and when it was full they took it to the mill.

"Now boys, you gonna have to git up 'bout 6:00 in the mornin' and I hate to get me a switch to get you up!"

But we be ready in the mornin' 'bout 5:30. He called that breakfast was ready with grits, eggs and 'em big ole biskits. My mamma even let us have a cuppa coffee.

"If you gonna work like a man, you should eat like one!" she said.

They built the fire under that big ole pot. My dad said he wanted it at 250° hot. They had to really clean the pot from leaves and dirt afore making the s'rup, so the water had to be really hot.

My dad had hitched that ole mule to the mill. They fed 'im real good that night before. Then they started 'im a walkin'' 'round and 'round.

Ralph lived across the way and was slow, but he was able to help some-times. He had got all the cane cut they had and put it in the truck and drove to the mill.

I told Byron, "I don't think we'll ever squeeze it all."

We started to put the cane in the mill. My dad had stretched a feed sack over a 55-gallon drum to catch whatever shouldn't go in the juice. He had a gourd dipper so's you could get a drink whenever you wanted one. It sure was sweet.

The mule was goin' 'round and 'round and every once in a while he'd fart. Boy! Was it loud!

After 'bout an hour we done squeezed a drum full. My dad got that ole bucket we used on wash day. He was puttin' that juice in the kit-tle. The ole mule was still goin' 'round and 'round but he warn't goin' nowhere.

My dad got what juice we had squeezed, enough to fill the kittle! We could see it boilin'. My dad had used 'em tree knots that me and Byron got over by the creek. Them thangs sure burn hot! My mama, she was skimmin' the foam and the dirt and the bad stuff off the top.

I hear tell if you feed that to the hogs that they get drunk. I wanted to do that so I can see it.

I saw my dad drop some water in the pot to see if it was ready. He got 'em liquor bottles from the Cane Patch Bar in Leesburg. There was some liquor left in 'em bottles and my dad said, "It give it a better taste." I'm not shore but what he drunk some of 'em before.

That white-lookin' stuff that we put in a bucket was sticky but tasted so good. It tastes even better the more you cook it to get the water out to make the s'rup. If you ain't never sopped a biskit in some good s'urp, you ain't lived.

We was still feedin' the cane to the mill. We'd gone through what was 1 wagon load and was 'bout 10:30. The first cookin' was comin' off. My mama had left and the other women too, to fix dinner. I told Byron that she was gonna bake some of 'em sweet taters jist the way he liked 'em. Byron said, "They ain't no way I don't like 'em. I could eat 'em three times a day."

They done got the wiskey bottles ready to go. My dad was dippin' and pourin' in 'em bottles. It sure looked good. One of my mama's biskits tastes so good on a cool day and warms you.

We was still grindin' and that ole feed sack got took over with a new one. When we jist 'bout grind all the cane and we was sticky as we could get, the day was comin' to an end.

They'd cooked all the juice we had. I was hungry enough to eat a hog. They had jist taken the last s'rup off but he left 'bout 2 gallon. My dad kept sturrin' so it wouldn't burn. I'll bet the ole mule was glad the day was over. They put 'im in the mule lot and he would root and kick. I don't know if he was jist so glad it was over or that he was dizzy.

My dad called, "Boys, come! This is what you're cookin'." It was like candy and we pulled and twisted and pulled and wrapped it around a tree limb. Then we layed it out to dry and he said, "You boys split it."

The day come to an end and we had to wash the cane off. It had been a hard day but we got it done. I bet 1 of 'em Yankees in New York never ever sopped a biskit. All my dad had ever seen 'em eat was that white store bread.

As everybody started to leave, my dad give 'em 1 of 'em wiskey bottles of s'rup.

Byron and myself, we jist layed down and didn't move 'til the sun come up the next mornin'.

Red and Byron

When Byron went to leave, my dad gave 'im 1 of 'em s'rups and my mama gave 'im a big sack of sweet taters.

Sure hope you have a friend like Byron has been to me.

Hog Cleanin'

Chapter 10

We always had hogs. Dad cooked 'bout every thin' that he fed the hogs. He would never be mean to the hog, dog, chicken or duck or nothin'. He didn't say much but when he did, I always knowed what he said, he meant!

Nearly every time the weather cooled he said, "We gonna clean hogs on Saturday. See if Byron can help." Ralph would be there and they could help scrape a small hog. So I stopped by Byron's to see if he could help and we went on to get Uncle Will. My dad could use his help too.

Uncle Will said, "Your pop done so much for me, I sure can be there Saturday mornin'."

We left Uncle Will's and walked by to Byron's house. He said, "Your mama gonna have some of 'em sweet taters for lunch? If she is, you know I'm gonna be here."

Byron spent Friday night with me so we could get up at 5:30 Saturday mornin'. We'd have breakfast my dad fixed. He always fixed breakfast. He had the wood stove goin' and built the fire around them 55-gallon drums. The water was almost boilin' but not hot enough yet. He cooked eggs and grits and ham and a big pot of coffee. And then he made 'em cat-eye biskits. They was the biggest biskits you ever did see and I like that.

Uncle Will come up and my dad told us to tell 'im to come inside and have breakfast.

Will said, "You sure he said that? I think I's better eat outside."

"Come on in, Will. We got a lotta work to do," Dad said.

My dad had done bought everybody a new knife and he made it so sharp you could shave with 'em. I couldn't; I ain't got no hair on my face. We all et all we could hold. Byron and me we had a cup of coffee with two spoons of sugar in it.

I took a look in the hog pen. He had three hogs to kill. It was gonna be a busy day!

The water was boilin' in that drum. My dad had 'bout twenty feed sacks. He put 'em in the three drums he had. He made a hook to get 'em sacks out of 'em drums. When the water got to boilin' hot, it was too hot! It set the hair, but he knowed jist how to do it.

The mornin' was cold. I said that it was too cold for me. My dad said, "If I put a belt on your behind you'll warm up." So I knowed not to say that again.

My dad told me to get the feed bucket; it had some corn in it. And then to get that big hog. He opened the gate; I lead that hog to where we was gonna scrape the hair off 'im.

My dad had a place layed out so it wouldn't be in the dirt. He lead that hog to it and gave Byron the .22 to kill the hog.

"Bam!" The hog was dead. Dad slit his throat so he would bleed out.

Then my dad hooked 1 of 'em hot sacks. It was what he layed the hog on to cool. "Get ready, boys!" Dad said. "Time to go to work."

We took 'em sharp knives and that hair come off easy in a few moments. He put another hot sack on that hog when we had 1 side done. We turned that hog over and did the other side. All the hair was gone. It didn't look bad; it was clean.

They cut the tendons on the hog legs so's they could hang it. We split it open to get the guts out. My dad saved the liver and heart. He put 'em guts in a wash tub, same wash tub I take a bath in. They took 'em on the porch and Miss Abby, the ole black lady who did the clothes washin', started cleanin' 'em chitlins to put the sage in. She turned it wrong side out and scraped 'em real good.

They didn't smell good yet but when they put that ole hog in it, it would be good. You could even sop it with some of that s'rup I like. They washed out the inside of that hog. They took them hams off; then took the hide off. My mama had a big fire on the wash pot, same pot we washed the clothes in.

They gave me a ham to cut the skin off. "Don't leave any meat on that fat! Jist the fat!" they said. We put the fat in a bucket. And, "Don't get none in the dirt." Byron had his done and I had mine done. My mama poured the fat in the wash pot.

Uncle Will had done them two shoulders while we done 1 shoulder, and he done his better than we done. They had the fire goin' in the smoke house. He hung 'em hams. My dad cut the meat off the rind; he cut the tenderloin out and give to my mama to cook for dinner. She had the wood stove goin' all mornin'.

She'd baked a cake and cooked a big batch of 'em sweet taters. She cooked 1 real big tater that Byron took. That back strap meat made some of them cat-eye biskits taste so good. We had a big pot of black-eyed peas. They was seven people helpin'. Lots of work! They had ice that day so we could have tea.

The wash pot was a-boilin' that lard, so we needed to dip it. They had 'bout five gallon cans. Byron got the dipper to dip the hot lard into the buckets. He filled three lard buckets. We took the dipper out and put the waste in an old tub to feed the hogs.

I cut the hog skin in 1-inch strips and then cut small pieces to put in the wash pot to start boilin'. It was cookin' the lard out of the hide. The hide would cook to the top. My dad took two boards with a thang to get the lard out of the skin. We put the skins in a flour sack; then we took the cracklin's inside 'em boards and squeezed the lard out.

They layed 'em out on a piece of tin to dry. My mama gave me a clean sack and told me to give some of 'em cracklin's to Byron. Byron heared what she said and said, "Hot dog!! We gonna have some cracklin' bread."

I took a hammer to the sack of cracklin's and beat the sack 'til they was broke up. Then I took it to the kitchen. It sure smelled good.

It was 'bout noon and my mama said that lunch was ready. So everyone washed up in the wash stand. A wash stand was a place with a pump and a pan to wash in and they was a gourd dipper if you needed a drink.

The table was set. They was seven of us and a place for only six, so Byron and I ate on the porch. They told Uncle Will to come inside but he said that he wanted to eat with his boys. So my mama fixed a big plate and gave Byron that big ole sweet tater. Everybody left to go back to work after they drank big glasses of sweet tea and ate a big piece of cake.

After we dipped the lard from the pot and put in the five gallon cans my mama told us to be sure to clean the pot. When we got it clean, we were to take some water from the drum and clean it real good. Then we turned it up-side-down and put the fire out.

Byron said, "That sweet tater shore filled me up." My dad told us we was through for the day and to go to the creek for a swim, but it was too cold.

My dad was cuttin' the hog head open so he could make hog head-cheese. That's brains. I don't think I want 'im to save some brains to cook in the mornin' with my eggs.

Byron said, "I think I'll go home. I'm tired."

My mama called Byron in the kitchen and gave 'im a big sack of sweet taters and a big piece of cake and a slice of cooked pork. She told 'im to sleep tight and not to let the bed bugs bite.

Ringworm

Chapter 11

Jist 'bout everybody had ground itch, called ringworm. Most of it come from cats and everybody had cats. Cats kept the rats away and we didn't need to feed 'em. They had to catch their own food.

Byron's sister, Melba, got ringworm on her rear end and scratched and scratched and scratched. Said she needed to have help to get rid of it. So Byron told her that there was somethin' in the barn that would kill it. We got some sand paper and sanded the ring worm and put some screwworm medicine on it! It warn't bad to start with, but afore long she was screamin' bloody murder!! I thought we killed her.

It had been rainin' and the clay road had water on it. She plumped her rear end in a mud hole to cool it off. In 'bout two days she showed to us. Sandin' had took the hide right off her rear end, but it killed that ringworm!

Stingin' Nettles, Plants and Bugs

Chapter 12

Stingin' Nettle is a plant with a little fuzz on the leaves. Sometimes when we'd get into one; it sure did hurt. But Uncle Will showed us what to do to get rid of the hurt. You pee on it and the sting would go away. 'Bout two or three feet down in the ground is a root that's good to eat.

They's a tree that grows in a fence row. It has thorns on it. If you pick some of that and put it inside your mouth for a bad toothache, it numbs it. But if you touch it with your tongue, it numbs it too.

They's another plant, don't smell too good, but would keep the skeeters off sometimes. The reason we had 'em tree houses twenty feet up, the skeeters warn't as bad up high.

And when it rained, them red bugs was bad!! We'd pour gas on 'em and set 'em on fire. When they moved, we'd stab 'em with an ice pick.

The Bees

Chapter 13

It was jist a lazy Saturday. Really nothin' to do so we was layin' up in the tree house hopin' maybe that snake would come by. Then we heared somethin' comin'. We knowed it warn't no snake, but maybe it was Bill.

But when he stepped out, it warn't Bill. It was R.H. That's what name he went by. He was a year older than me. He had a hammer with 'im. Said, "I'm gonna get me some honey down at the spring".

I said, "You know who owns them bees?"

"Nope," he said.

"What if'n you get caught?" we asked.

"Ain't gonna get caught; they's all gone. I done looked," he said.

So we climb down. He was dipping snuff. He always dipped snuff. Byron said, "Give me a dip."

So he pulled his lip out and poured some in Byron's mouth. Then Byron coughed and there was snuff everywhere. We went down to Bugg Spring to wash his mouth out so he could finally breathe right.

R.H asked me if I wanted some.

"Nope" I said, "jist give my snuff to Byron. He likes it better'n I do."

We left Bugg Spring Run headin' south through the swamp and to wade some water. We had to watch out for snakes though. Them snakes in the swamp, they don't let you know when they're there. The only way you can tell is that you smell 'em. They smell like someone that never takes a bath. They stink!

We seen the bamboo by the springs and knowed the beehive was near by. We got some pine straw, put it in the smoker. Byron had the smoker goin'. I took R.H.'s hammer, opened the top of the box.

R.H. was pickin' them Spanish seed off'n 'im.

Byron smoked them bees.They was flyin' everywhere.He got 'im some honey cone and I got me some cone. We put the top back on. I hit the top of the box and that made them bees mad!!

R.H said, "Gimme my hammer".

So I gave it to 'im. Byron poured them pine needles in the smoker to put the fire out so it could be put back in the barn.

I told Byron, "We need to get out of here." So we headed back through the swamp. We heared R.H. hollerin'. Them bees had done ate 'im up. They was mad when he opened the top! We didn't see 'im then for a while.

Later we saw 'im at the store and he said them bees like to eat 'im alive. He was stung 'bout ten times and they shore did hurt. "I should have run like you did and I wouldna got stung," he said.

I sure didn't tell 'im I was the cause of 'im gettin' stung!

The honey was green. The bees hadn't capped the top of the hive with wax yet. And if you ate green honey it give you the back-door trots. It put us in the woods with some moss.

Back to School and the Swamp

Chapter 14

Come Monday mornin' I went to school. I didn't want to, but I went. I went over there and we had a new teacher. I didn't like that new teacher; I liked that ole teacher. I was in love with her. She was beautiful. This woman was purty old. But I knowed I had to go, so I went.

And the school was not too far, so I'd walk over there. We got there and she told us what her name was and school got goin'.

My brother was the school janitor. He was in the eighth grade. Well, he expected me to go there and help 'im clean that school up. He got five dollars a month. Expected me to help but he didn't want to give me no money. My mama expected me to help 'im. I said, "He don't pay me nothin' and he gets paid."

She said, "Well, go there and help 'im anyways."

I said, "No. No. I'll get me a job pickin' tomatoes or whatever."

So she said, "Ok."

But he still had me come over there and move all 'em desks around so he could come in and mop the floor and clean the bathrooms. He wanted me to clean 'em bathrooms, and I didn't want to clean 'em. So we went to school the whole week, got over there on Friday and I told Byron, "Saturday mornin', what you want to do?"

He said, "Well, let's go see if we can see that snake."

I said, "Ok. Well, I'll be at your house 'bout 7:30 or 7 o'clock."

He said, "That'll be fine."

So I went by Byron's and he said, "You know, my mama told me I gotta get rid of my goat."

I said, "What?"

He said, "Yeah. That goat got out and pulled the clothes down and got the wash clothes filthy as they could be. My mama told me if I don't get rid of that goat, then I'll be doin' the washin' and I don't want to do no washin'." They didn't even have nothin' to wash with 'cept a scrub board like the rest of us. And they was a big family then. That washin' woulda took 'im two days to do.

So he said, "I gotta get rid of my goat."

I said, "Why don't you take 'im to Uncle Will?"

He said, "Yeah, I could do that. You know it's fixin' to have babies."

I said, "It is?"

He said, "Yeah. You want one?"

I said, "No, I don't want one. That thang'd pull my mama's clothes down off the line and she'd beat me with 1 of 'em switches in the yard."

He said, "Ok. I'll get a rope and put it 'round that goat's neck; we'll take it over there and give it to Uncle Will." He said, "One day we'll eat it."

And I said, "That's fine with me."

So we went over there to Uncle Will's and come up with that goat. He had a little pen there and we said, "You can put it in that pen, Uncle Will. It'll eat grass and it'll eat 'most anythin'."

He said, "Where'd you boys get that-there goat?"

We said, "It was runnin' 'round loose, so we thought you could have it. And its fixin' to have babies and you could milk that thang."

He said, "I don't want that goat there, boys. If someone find this goat he'll think I took it and he'll jist shoot an ole black man like me. You don't understand. You white boys don't know what it's like to be black."

"Yeah, but Uncle Will, we want you to have this goat; ain't nobody gonna bother you."

He said, "You stole my chickens and then you ate 'em. Then you turned 'round and stole somebody else's chickens and put 'em in my pen. Then you had to take 'em chickens back and you got another chicken from somewhere and you put it in my pen! Boys, you don't understand." Said, "An ole black man like me jist can't go out there and steal stuff. I ain't never stole nothin' in my life! Y'all stealing everythin'.

You stole a man's milk. I don't know what to do with you."

"Well," Uncle Will said, "I'm not keepin' it. If anyone asks, it's not mine." He said, "Where you boys headed?"

We said, "Over to the swamp."

He said, "I sure would like a couple of squirrels."

We said, "Ok, we can get you a couple of squirrels."

He said, "Alright, I'll put the goat in the pen and I'll feed 'im."

Byron said, "You can milk 'im too!"

We eased on down the trail, got over there on the road to the hammock. He says, "You want to go to Cason Hammock or want to go to the Denham Swamp?"

I said, "Well, let's walk over the grove and see what we see." We seen a track goin' which-a-way, and you could tell which way that snake crawls. So we went on over the edge of the swamp. We jist had a feelin' that somethin' warn't quite what it ought to be. We jist had this feelin'. I knowed it. I feel it.

Byron said, "Think it's the snake?"

I said, "I don't know what it is but I feel it. Somethin's here."

So he said, "Alright." He took the safatey off his .45-70 and we was walkin' along there. We stopped dead in our tracks. You ain't never gonna guess what was standin' there—Uncle Will!

We said, "Uncle Will, what are you doin' down here?"

He said, "Boys, that snake went by my house after y'all left and I wanted to make sure he hadn't got y'all."

"He went by your house?"

"Yeah, he went by my house. He was crawlin' fast. He didn't even slow up!"

We said, "Well, why didn't you shoot 'im?"

He said, "I'm afraid to shoot 'im. If I miss 'im, he'll kill me."

We said, "Which way did he head?"

He said, "He headed towards Cason Hammock." So we run. We run down where the road is comin' in, jumped the fence, went up there and climbed in our tree stand. The woods was deathly quiet.

We said, "He's here. He's here."

We eased around and we looked. There warn't a sound in that swamp. It was quiet. It was scary. We listened for somethin', lookin' to see a leaf move, a tree move. Not a sound or a thang; jist quiet. I made sure that I layed my bullets out where I could get to 'em if I needed another immediately. We heared a noise.

I said, "Is that snake under this tree?"

"I don't know," Byron said. Then we heared a noise, and then it got quiet. He was over to the left. Then all of a sudden he was over to the right.

Said, "What do you think it is?"

"Don't know." It was startin' to rain a little bit, but we stayed dry underneath that roof we'd built.

Said, "Do you hear that noise?"

"Yeah."

"What is it?"

"I don't know."

I said, "You know, you still smell like a polecat!"

He jist laughed. "Gotta be that snake. But they ain't two of 'em in here." Then we heared the noise on two sides. "And that's it. He's comin', through." Then, in steps a sow with its four little piggies.

He said, "But there's somethin' on the left side too."

So we watched her and we said, "That snake is after her or them piggies. He wants to eat one of 'em piggies."

Uncle Will and the Goats

Chapter 15

Well, we got back there. This big ole hog, he come out and he was huge!

Byron said, "You want me to kill 'im?"

I said, "No, don't kill 'im. He ain't no good for nothin'. Them boar hogs, all they do is stink up the woods." Them hogs, they had these big old shields on the sides, them teeth on the front and you could see 'im grittin' 'em teeth.

Byron said, "I need be goin' home."

I said, "What you want me to do?"

He said, "Shoot a hole through that hog's ear." He got 'bout 50 yards out there. I go down in the position and "POW!" You could see the bullet make a hole in his ear. They was a little bit of blood but that ole hog, he make a sound so loud it go all through the woods, and the pigs go one way and he go the other. There's squallin' and hollerin' and runnin'. And I'd never see such sounds goin' on in all my life. Then it got quiet.

So we said, "Aw, let's go to Uncle Will's."

So we went down to Uncle Will's and went through Stage Coach Road and cut by his house. He was sittin' outside smokin' his pipe. Well, he layed it down and we got us a drag from it. We said, "Uncle Will, how's the goat goin'?"

He said, "Oh, you boys need to see this."

He'd built an ole shed out of some tin for the goat to go under when it rained. Goats don't like rain. And they get pneumonia real easy and then they die. There was two little ole nanny goats 'bout the size of a big rooster. And they was purty as they could be.

We said, "You gonna milk the goat?"

He said, "I ain't gonna milk it 'til we wean them goats off. When they start eatin' grass, well, I'll wean 'em and I'll get the milk."

We said, "You want us to take some boards over here and build a thang to sit on so you won't have to squat?"

He said, "Yeah, that'd be good, boys."

I said, "That goat ain't got no teeth!"

He said, "Yeah, he does."

I said, "No he don't."

He said, "Well, he don't have teeth on the top and on the bottom like you do. He has 1 set of teeth. And then he got a hard plate on the top."

We said, "Oh, Ok. Them sure are purty, Uncle Will."

He said, "Well, ain't nobody come to claim 'em yet." But he said, "If they do, I'm gone. I ain't gonna get shot over no goat."

"Well," we said, "Will, we gonna cut across here and see what we find." Said, "We didn't see no tracks of the big snake. He jist ain't in that swamp."

He said, "Why don't you two find somethin' else to do besides go to that swamp? That place is a dangerous place. There's big ole gators in it too. Y'all done kill all 'em ole wild dogs." Said, "There's more rattle-snakes in that place than you can shake out a thicket."

We said, "Well, we killed quite a few of 'em. We's workin' on 'em. We can get a whole dollar for their skins. We done saw big ole hog there on Thursday. We seen a sow and her pigs."

He said, "I seen them pigs 'cause they come 'round here. Can you shoot 1 of 'em for me?"

We said, "We can do that. That big ole boar hog, he got shields on his sides and he looks bad. We let 'im go. We didn't shoot 'im 'cause we didn't want to clean 'im. And if we ain't gonna clean 'im, then they ain't no use in shooting 'im.

He said, "Well, boys, that's right." Said, "Let the stuff lives that needs to live." Said, "Lord put 'im there, and the Lord will take 'em away if they get bad."

Said, "Well, you know we're at school now and we can't come down here and hunt every day for that snake."

He said, "Well, that's probably good."

Betty Jean

Chapter 16

Betty Jean was Byron's sister, 'bout 2 years older than Byron.

The thang I remember most 'bout Betty Jean is the time we was eatin' mulberries. Now when you eat mulberries, you gotta blow on 'em first to get the bugs out. They was lots and lots of bugs in that-there tree.

One day while we was all up in the tree eatin' mulberries, Betty Jean slipped and fell a bit. She hung by her foot and we couldn't lift her up to get her foot loose.

Byron said, "I know, I can shoot her out." So he went in to get his gun, but Melba told her mama what he was gonna do. 'Course his mama come out and she told 'im he couldn't do that and that we would hafta get together and lift her out.

We did got her out and she was skinned, but not really hurt bad.

The Rosewall School

Chapter 17

The Rosewall School is still standin' today. This was the school for the black children so they could learn to read and write, too. They couldn't go to the same school as us white kids.

The school was in the Quarters with the black people. Not sure how many grades it had, but everyone needed to learn to read and write. My daddy, he couldn't read and write in the early 1900's. They went to work, not school. If'n it warn't for Mr. Rosewall, there would be a lot of good people who couldn't read and write.

'Bout 15 years ago now, the volunteer fire department rebuilt it. But it's in bad shape again.

Rosewall School as it looks now, in 2016

The Pocketbook

Chapter 18

This was 1 of 'em days with nothin' goin' on and not a thang to do. So, we was down in the hog pen. The weather looked bad. We tried to stay out of the swamp in bad weather.

Byron asked Betty Jean if she had an old pocketbook. She said she did but she wanted to go with us, and asked us, "What you gonna do with it?"

Said, "We gonna pull a pocketbook." So we got a strong string and put some moss in the pocketbook to fill it up.

"Let's go by the school down by the railroad track."

Catfish Larry, a kid we went to school with, Melba, Byron, Betty Jean and me, we took off down the clay road. We went by the store, put all our money together and got one of 'em big Black Cow candy bars. And everybody got a mouthful.

We went through the woods to stay off the road. They was a ditch by the side of the road 'bout 3 foot deep. We put the pocket book in the middle of the road and had the string tied to the pocketbook. It looked good.

They was a car comin' down the road. Byron had the string. We had to hide so's the driver couldn't see us. We was laughin'. The car stopped to get the pockatebook. But when the fellow reached for it, Byron pulled the string. He run tryin' to get it and then he saw us!!

He called us some bad thangs before gettin' back in his car.

So we put it back in the middle of the road. I saw Homer and his wife, Faye, comin'. She said, "Stop, Homer! They's a pocketbook in the road." They was ridin a Model A "Goat".

He told Faye, he said, "You better leave that thang alone."

"Stop! Homer. I want it," she said.

He stopped and she reached for the pocketbook. Byron moved it and she jumped three feet in the air. Homer laughed. He took out his pistol and shot in the air. We all run ever which way. I run and hid in the packin' house. I dunno where the others went.

In 'bout 20 minutes they all come back and we had a good laugh.

We put the pocketbook back in the middle of the road and stopped four or five more cars. Some of 'em people laughed and some said bad thangs to us.

We had it in the middle of the road and we saw a car comin' but was too late. Byron done pulled real quick, but we was caught. The patrolman had done caught us. Betty, Catfish, Larry, they run. Byron and me was caught. He put us in the back seat of the car and told us he was gonna take us to jail! We would get 20 years, maybe more! I thought I'd be old and gray by then.

He told us that if we could pay 'im $100 he would let us go. He pulled under the oak at the school and opened the back door to let the cool air in. I looked at Byron and he said, "RUN!"

We jumped out the back door and run as fast as we could. The patrolman blew his siren! It sure was loud. I run as fast as I could. We hid under the depot for 'bout an hour. He drove by once. I didn't want to go to no jail for 20 years.

We went over to Byron's house. My heart was a thumpin' loud. I asked Byron, "Do you think he'll bring them dogs out to find us? Maybe we should get our gun, jist in case."

The next day was a school day. I didn't want to go to school. That lawman come to school I was gonna jump out the window and go to Denham Swamp. He won't never find me there for years later.

Years later, as an adult, I was a mechanic and had my own station. I was workin' on that same patrolman's car. When he returned to get his car I asked 'im if he remembered when he caught two boys in Okahumpka pullin' a "pocketbook".

He said, "Yes, I remember and I never laughed so much 'bout anythin'. I bet you didn't pull no "pocketbook" after that!

And we didn't.

Religion and Inoculations

Chapter 19

We left Uncle Will's, and Byron went home and I went on home. I got there and my mama jist fixed supper. I sat down and et supper. We had cornbread, lima beans; had a big ole bass. Whew! that thang good. My dad caught 'im over there in Lake Harris. My brother was jokin' around somewhere.

I hung my hat on the horn like my dad did. He'd give me his ole Stetson hat and I had to put newspaper in it to build it out so it'd fit my head.

Dad said, "What 'bout that big snake over there in the swamp? Do you know anythin' 'bout it?"

I said, "I seen it twice, but it was always runnin' so fast."

He said, "I heared they's some hogs over there too."

I said, "Yes, sir, they is. They're some small pigs over there proba-bly 'bout 20 pounds. When they get to be 'bout 60 pounds we'll get 1 of 'em."

He said, "That's fine. That's fine." He said, "Do you know where to shoot 'im?"

I said, "Yeah. Shoot 'im in the head so it don't mess up the ribs."

He said, "That's right."

It was gettin' a little chilly. So I sat down by the fireplace and watched the flicker of the fire. I don't know if you ever set by the fireplace or not. Well, you warm 1 side and turn 'round and warm the other side. By the time you do that, the other side is cold again. But it's better than nothin'. Then I went to bed. My brother come in 'bout 11 o'clock and sticked his cold feet next to me. I thought, *I'll get even with you some day.*

Then daylight come and I got up, got ready and went to church and listened to the preacher preach. The church down there got cracks in the floor, so you could look and see the dogs down underneath there. And whenever we couldn't make us enough money to get us a can of Prince Albert and 1 of 'em Black Cow candy bars, we'd get up under the church with a piece of hardware cloth and a shovel. We'd scoop up under where they took the collection and get a nickel or a dime or a few pennies off the ground.

It was cold in the winter time there and they had a woodstove. They built a fire and the people set 'round the fire. The preacher got up and preached. They was probably 15 -20 people there. We had little wooden benches to sit on. It was still a good place to go. Well, we joined the church. Byron and I both thought we'd join. I guess we needed to.

We went down to Bright Lake and they baptized us. We took off our shoes, 'cause we didn't want to get our shoes wet. And we was sittin' on the back of a tailgate on a truck on the way down. They went down and baptized us and they baptized Betty Jean too.

Comin' back we put our tennis shoes on and we dragged 'em on the highway. They'd smoke and get so hot we had to lift 'em off the highway, and then my mama tore my behind up. Them shoes cost a dollar!! My dad made 'bout ten dollars a week. He took my shoes to the blacksmith shop and had 'im put some leather soles on them thangs. He put them thangs on with a cross stitch. I liked that. I had the only pair of leather tennis shoes there was. All I really wanted was a pair of 'em Red Rider tennis shoes. They cost two dollars and my shoes only cost 1 dollar. But I wanted a pair of 'em Red Riders. My mama wouldn't get 'em 'cause they cost too much.

Red Ryder Tennis Shoes

We went back to school on Monday mornin' and they informed us that they were gonna give us an inoculation. Well, I'd never had 1 of 'em. I didn't know what it was. So I said, "Byron, what's an inoculation?"

He said, "I don't know. I never had 1 either."

Well, we had a new boy that come to school there this year. His name was Joe. We said, "Joe, what is an inoculation?" He didn't know neither.

The next day the Health Department come out there to give us an inoculation and we found out that it was a shot. "Whew Doggie!!" I said, "I don't want no shot!" But I had to take a paper home and my mama signed it and I took it back. It was for smallpox and for measles. "I done had the measles," I said. Well, we got our shot!!

Joe, he jumped out the window and he went home. I said, "His mama's gonna beat 'im, Whew Doggie!" Well, he come back to school the next day and she hadn't beat 'im. We thought, *Hmm*.

The teacher told us that everybody got their inoculation for the day, all except Joe. His mama said he didn't have to take it.

That sounded purty good to me. I wish my mama said I didn't have to get it, 'cause I didn't want it. And when they stuck that needle in me, I wanted to scream bloody murder, but I didn't do it. I was too pepped up to do that.

Christmas and New Year

Chapter 20

We was standin' there in the classroom and everythin' was goin' along good. All of a sudden we saw a bunch of cows run by the window. We all run to the window to watch. Teacher run and locked the doors. It was a stampede. They's a loadin' pen right down there by the depot and 'em cows decided to run! They didn't run very far. I thought a stampede must have been for a hundred miles, but cows can't run that long.

The cowboys finally rounded 'em up and the teacher, she opened the doors. We all wondered if she locked 'em doors so 'em cows couldn't get in the school, or was she locking 'em doors to keep us from gettin' out of the school. We didn't ask her though 'cause the new teacher didn't give much answers.

They was 1 Friday when Byron and I decided we jist didn't want to go to class. So we put on that we was sick. We had a stomach ache. Somethin' we done et give us a stomach ache.

They was a bed in a little room with a door so we went over and layed in that bed. She closed the door. Well, we stayed there 'bout two hours or maybe three hours. We didn't hear no noise. They's always some kind of noise goin' on in that classroom. Didn't hear nothin'. So we opened the door and saw that everybody was gone but us! They'd went on a field trip. And 'cause we was "sick" we didn't get to go!

I looked at Byron and said, "We done missed that field trip!"

He said, "I didn't know, and I'd rather be there than here."

Well, it be gettin' on Christmas time and they decided they'd have a Christmas tree. She said, "Boys, can you go get us a Christmas tree?"

We said, "Sure can."

We go down there on the east side of Bugg Spring and we can cut 1 of 'em trees down there. So we went by the store afore we went down by the Spring and bought us a package of Pall Mall cigarettes and some matches. They was 'bout 15 cents. We scraped all the money we could get and we lit ourselves a cigarette. We was goin' down the road and we passed the wrong person! We passed Miss Sally! We all loved her. She was such a nice lady. (She was the Postmaster later on in life.) Her mama was the Postmaster then. She went right down and told our teacher that we was smokin'. All of us, all five of us.

So, no big deal. We thought maybe the teacher'd give us 50 cents for that Christmas tree.

We went down over the edge of the hammock there by the pine trees. We cut the pine tree down. We didn't know much 'bout Christmas trees. Didn't know what made much difference. So we cut it down and then we couldn't carry the thang. So we dragged it and we smoked all that pack of cigarettes. We got down to the road down there and we dragged it down the road. It was hard draggin'. We got all that pine sap on us.

We got to the school and we had dragged off 1 side off that tree! So they had to stand it in the corner to hide the bare side. One of the men down there he built a thang to stand the tree in.

The teacher come out and wanted to know who bought them cigarettes. Ain't nobody said nothin', so she jist whipped all five of us for smokin'. She said, "I've got a mind to tell your mamas. But I won't have to 'cause y'all smell like cigarettes!"

Well, on the way home, me and Byron done been down that road before. So we stopped by a comphor tree and we got 'em camphor leaves and chewed up a whole bunch of 'em. We could tell our mamas that we was burning camphor to keep 'em skeeters off. The camphor leaves didn't keep the skeeters off but it made you smell like camphor.

I got home and my mama gave me a dose of somethin'. It was castor oil. I hated that stuff! Whew! I hated it. She said, "That'll get all the nicotine out of your system."

I didn't know what nicotine was. She said, "I don't want to hear no more of this smokin' cigarettes. I don't care if you're smokin' rabbit tobacco, but I don't want to see you smokin' no more cigarettes."

Well, they decorated the tree. They made popcorn and they put on pinecones and all of this and that. They had a beautiful Christmas tree and they had a Christmas program over there. The teacher gave us a pencil for Christmas. That was my first Christmas present I ever got. It was a pencil, but I really wanted a Red Rider wagon. I didn't get it. But I kept that pencil for years.

After Christmas it was New Year comin' along. It was a dead winter that year. They planted the crops early and they froze. They went on and they saw that they warn't gonna be able to plant the watermelons like they did. My dad went on to work for some construction company as a guard. He made two dollars a night and that was more'n what he was makin' before.

Rabbit Tobacco

Back to the Hunt

Chapter 21

The summer come along. My daddy quit that job and went back to farmin' again. He was growin' taters and peas and corn and havin' to work the fields. School finally let out and we went after that snake again. We gonna kill the snake this time. That thang's worth a hundred dollars, and we ain't never had a hundred dollars. We'd skinned gators and we'd done other thangs and we worked every time we could find a job. We worked down at the dairy washin' bottles and sweepin' floors and anythin' that we could do.

So we went over to the swamp and somebody'd tore our spot up! We thought it was probably Bill. Well, we had to rebuild it, 'cause we needed it to watch for thangs below! We started gatherin' up wood and sticks, went over and re-built the platform. Then we got us some more tin and put up the mattress made out of grass. It'd been wet so many times it was like layin' on a board.

So we got us some new sacks, went out there in the field behind Uncle Will's and filled them sacks up with grass. That took us two days! We was layin' up there one day and you know what? Byron said, "We need to shoot Bill!" Said, "Yeah, shot a hole in his ear to let 'im know what we think of 'im!"

I said, "No, they'll put us in jail. 'I don't think we'd better shoot Bill." He said, "Well, Ok."

We was layin' up in there 1 Saturday and he said, "You know what? This old snake is smart as he can be, but he ain't as smart as we are. Why don't you bring that cur dog of yours over here and we'll try to get that snake whenever we find it."

I said, "I'll do it."

We called 'im, "Old Yeller." I got up and got Old Yeller. It was Monday mornin'. I took 'im over to Uncle Will's. He said, "Boys, what you gonna do with that-there dog?"

We said, "We find that snake trail, we gonna put Old Yeller on it."

He said, "Y'all don't know. You put that dog on that trail, that snake will kill that dog. You don't know what you're foolin' with. That thang is bad; he run faster than a racehorse. And he knows these woods and he got them trails everywhere."

"We'll go over there to Lake Denham Swamp and take Old Yeller over there." Said, "We'll take 'im up in the treehouse with us. We'll put 'im in a sack and put 'im up there."

He said, "That's a purty big job to put a dog in a sack that don't wanta be there."

But we got 'im in there. We got 'im and layed 'im up on our platform. He layed down. We layed there for 3-4 hours with nothin' happenin'. Seen an old moccasin down there. Seen an eagle flyin', a fish eagle. It'd caught it a fish. Seen a couple of squirrels run up and down a tree. Seen a couple of coons wash their food. We thought that's why they did, to clean it, but what they did was soften it up so they could eat it.

So we was 'bout to get down and leave when we hear this noise comin'. The dog started to bark, but I slapped 'im upside the head to shut 'im up. And there walked out that old boar hog again. He was a gruntin' and a groanin'.

Byron said, "Look where you hit 'im in the ear. He look bad, don't he?"

He's a bad hog. He had 'em old tusks on the front and them thangs is bad, bad news. Them thangs will cut you on the front, cut you wide open. He'd kill this dog here.

Byron said, "Put another hole in his ear."

So I layed there and "POW!" That old hog jumped and ran right into the trees and he tore down through that swamp. You could hear 'im runnin' through that water and mud. That's the last time we ever saw 'im. I knowed we didn't hit 'im in the head. I only hit 'im in the ear. But I figured he didn't want no more of that part of the country. We had seen them pigs, but they was too far away to shoot. These pigs had grown up to 'bout 60-80 pounds. And both of us could carry out 1 of 'em hogs. We'd gut 'im out, cut his head off, and then he wouldn't be too heavy. So we was tryin' to get us 1 of them, but we never did come close enough.

That old dog he wanted to get down there. So we got 'im in the sack again. That was an education to put 'im back in the sack! It was some-thin'!! He didn't want to go in, so we put it over his head first and then tied the sack. We got 'im on the ground and held 'im off the ground jist long enough so we could get down there and get a rope on 'im 'cause we knowed he'd run off.

We left there and went back out to the edge of the orange grove, walked back up to Cason Hammock, and there it was! It was 'bout 4:30 in the afternoon and we thought it was too late to put the dog on 'im today. There we done seen our snake. We'd made a mistake again. We'd went to Cason Hammock instead of the swamp. But that warn't the first mistake we made. So we thought we'd never get 'im. But we was gonna kill that snake. We gotta get 'im 'cause he's worth a hundred dollars! And we ain't never had no hundred dollars before. We want that snake.

School had been out for a couple of months. We'd go down there every day and sit and wait. I had the dog and decided to go over to By-ron's to see if he could go, and he could. He had his old .45-70 and I had my .22. We eased down through the woods and we found his track, and I put the dog on 'im. The dog trailed 'im. The dog stopped and I said, "Oh, My! He's right on top of us, Byron. That old snake is right out in front of us and he's right on top of us. If he runs at us, don't you miss!!"

He said, "I won't." I tell you what, the sweat was pouring off me. It looked like it'd rained on me. I said, "There he is! Kill 'im!"

He said, "If he moves, then I'll see his head and he'll be a dead snake!"

I tell 'im, "Ok." The old dog was over there tryin' to get to where it was. Low and behold! Guess what? Out walks that big ole boar hog again.

Byron says, "See 'im?"

I said, "Yeah."

He says, "You want me to kill 'im?"

I thought, *You know what? That old boar hog is either after that snake or that snake is after that boar hog. If that boar hog gets 'im before we do, he'll tear the hide up on 'im, but the snake'll kill 'im.*

I said, "No, don't kill 'im; he'll jist stink up the woods."

So we turned around and left. Went back down to Uncle Will's and he was sittin' there milkin' the goat. He'd milked that thang jist 'bout all winter long. He was drinkin' that goat milk. He said it was good for his stomach. He'd drink that shine, too, and that was bad for his stomach. He done drunk all that wine that we made.

Pokeberry Injuns, Doggone
Chapter 22

We said, "You know what? Them Injuns, they got red skin on 'em. And 'cause they got red skin, they say animals don't see 'em."

I don't know if you ever seen a pokeberry or not. But them pokeberries grow in the woods. So we went over to where they was, 'bout 4-5 bushes of them thangs and we picked 'em. Our hands turned red, but we still picked 'em. We take our shirts off, but I sunburn so bad I had to put mine back on. We put them pokeberries all over our face, our arms and our whole bodies from the waist up. And we was Injuns!

We was Injuns like you ain't never seen afore. We was barefoot like 'em. We could go through the woods like 'em, and now we was red-skinned, so them varmints couldn't see us! We gonna get that snake now 'cause he can't see us!

So we went back over in there the next mornin', took the dog with us, found that track. He'd took toward Cason Hammock.

Byron said, "Turn the dog loose."

And he let out a howl. He run in there and run into the bottom of the swamp where them burnt-out stumps was. I heared 'im squeal and then nothin'. Byron, said, "What happened?"

I said, "I don't know. He would have howled if he'd got that snake!" So we eased down through the swamp to where we thought he was at. We saw the big snake's track. I looked and my dog was dead.

That snake done stabbed 'im with them fangs. They'd done gone all the way through my dog's head and come out the bottom. And the snake was gone!

I said, "He killed my dog."

Byron said, "Well, what are you gonna do with the dog?"

I said, "I'll jist leave 'im be. Some varmint will come here and eat 'im. And that'll be alright."

I was sad 'bout losin' my dog, but I understand that if I hadn't turned 'im loose, it might have been us that the snake got. I'd rather he got the dog than us. We went back and crawled up onto our platform. We layed up in our grass bed.

"You know what? This sure is a fine place to rest, isn't it?"

He said, "Yeah, it is. I love this swamp. I love Uncle Will," and I said, "I do too."

He said, "You know what? Uncle Will's old."

I said, "Yeah, yeah."

He said, "He don't know how old he is. He don't know where he was born. So if we ask 'im, he jist says he don't know."

I said, "He worked around here all his life."

'Bout Watermelons

Chapter 23

He said, "Yeah, you know the summer is here now and the watermelons is comin' in next week? Are we gonna work in the watermelons?"

I said, "Yeah, we gonna work in the watermelons."

So we climbed down out of our tree and went down to the store. There was a man down there huntin', and he said he'd give us a penny a watermelon to take and load them up.

I didn't know how to swim. I'd been all over them marshes, but didn't know how to swim. I told Byron, I said, "I don't know how to swim."

He said, "Well, someday I'll teach you."

I said, "Ok."

Well, we're out there in that field in that hot sunshine and he said, "Let's go swimmin' in the creek."

I said, "I don't know how to swim, 'member?"

He said, "I'll teach you."

Well, there's holes in that creek. And whenever we got to 1 of them holes he'd drag me through or I'd swim through. In 'bout a week I swam 'bout as good as anybody else could.

And we carried 'em watermelons out. We'd carry 'bout 1 and then ten. He'd pay us a dollar a day for what we'd do. Then we went to the boxcars and we'd label watermelons and get 'bout 25 cents a rail car. We could do 'bout 3 of 'em a day and maybe 4 sometimes. There was a light-colored fella there that worked for Byron's dad. They called 'im "Frog."

Well, Frog had stole 'im 2 watermelons out there from a boxcar. He was gonna take them watermelons and sell 'em or do somethin' with them. And Byron and I found 'im. So what we did, we cut them watermelons open and made us a helmet like them football players wear and stuck them thangs on our head. Watermelon juice is really sticky, but that was alright. And we wore them thangs around for 'bout two or three days. Frog got some kind of mad, but he couldn't say nothin', 'cause he done stole them and we'd took 'em away from 'im.

Every day whenever the train would come by, there was a feller workin' in the baggage part of the train, and you'd get these watermelons and you'd sell them to 'im. You'd get 'bout ten cents apiece for 'em. Well, you'd go up there to that boxcar and guess what he'd do? Jist as the train would come around he'd say "Boys, now give me that watermelon there and I'll give you a dime." Well, you'd run that watermelon over there and he'd jist wave at you!!

He did that two or three times and we thought, *Well, this time we'll fix 'im!* So we took us 1 of them watermelons and cut the plug out and we took all the watermelon out of it. We went down there to the dairy and filled that thang plum full of wet cow manure and put that plug back in. Such a stink in there!! It held the plug!! And we waited for the train man. I was standin' there lookin' for the dime and he said, "Put it right there." Byron lifted that thang up and threwed it. The cow manure went all over inside that boxcar!!!

The next day he had a man with a badge on there. He said, "I understand you boys throwed a watermelon full of cow manure on the train."

We said, "Yes, sir, we did." And then we told 'im 'bout what the train man would do with us all the time. So he went and got 'im and brought 'im down there.

One of the men that was down there at the boxcar had seen 'im do it a couple of times to other people and us too. And he said, "That's right, that's right. He done it to 'em."

He fired the train man on the spot. And we walked off down the road. I told Byron, I said, "You know we coulda went to jail!"

He said, "Ah, well that's alright. We'd have been in there together." I took that as a real nice compliment!

We was hangin' around the boxcars and workin' wherever we could and they would pay us a little bit. Then the OPA (Office of Price Administration) would come in and they would price this stuff. You couldn't sell it so high a price. They had an old man who drove a Hudson car and he was over that part of it. In other words, if they thought somebody was chargin' too much, then they would fine you for it. I think he was workin' on a percentage. If they started sellin' watermelon down by the depot and he was up there by the store, one of them salesmen that was sellin' it would say, "Here boys, here's 50 cents; let the air out of his tires."

We'd let two of 'em out, then the only way he could get it back up was to take his tire pump and pump it back up. We'd put the pump up on the woods and then we'd leave.

So the fella said, "Go down and let the air outta his tires."

Byron'd get on 1 side and I'd get the other. I looked over there and the old man was beatin' Byron with a cane. But Byron was still unscrewin' that valve. He took the valve and layed it up there on the hood. Now the old feller could hardly walk; he had bad feet or bad legs or somethin', but he chased 'im up there. He was chasin' Byron 'round the car and I ran.

We got back to the boxcar and Byron said, "Doggone, for a quarter, we did that!!??"

I said, "Yeah, how many quarters we made that we didn't get beat for with a cane?"

He said, "But you ain't got beat with a cane."

I said, "I know."

We was good friends and I appreciated it. We worked in the boxcars and I would put the boards in the door; we label the light skins or blue skins. Then we walked up and down the tracks. We decided that we'd take and go out to Red Hill Grove; that's the dirt road goin' toward Sumterville.

We walked out to the grove and they told us that they was prunin' some trees. We went after them orange trees for a couple of days and they paid us purty good. They'd give us 'bout 2 dollars a day for prunin' them trees. It was how many trees you could prune a day.

So my dad sharpened our prunin' saws up for us and we went out and pruned. Took me a fish for dinner and two biscuits with some jelly on 'em. And we had an ole glass jug of water and we'd wrap towels 'round it and set it in the pond so that it would stay cool. Well, we worked there for three or four days, but the man didn't think we was doin' it fast enough so he told us not to come back. We decided if we went back we'd jist walk through the woods down to the spring and walk through there. We'd go by where the spring is and look at the spring and then go on down.

Well, we went through there, and went to the first grove, and went to the second grove; and walkin' along the edge of the hammock we'd walk by and always run into the Lake Denham Swamp. We went on down 'bout 200 yards and if that snake warn't there!! That's the first time we had been at the point where, ifn we'd had our rifle, we coulda have killed it. It saw us and it lit out, and it was runnin'!! If he'd have run at us there wouldn't have been nothin' we could have done.

So we come on down Stagecoach Road, cut through the trail, and went by Uncle Will's house. Uncle Will was in there cookin' supper. He was cookin' some grits and eggs, and we told 'im 'bout the snake. He said, "Boys! That snake could've killed y'all. You need to stay out of that-there swamp!"

We left Uncle Will's and walked back across the field and waded across the marsh. I said, "I'll see you tomorrow, Byron. I'm goin' home."

I went on home and I got there in time for supper. We sat down and had supper. My daddy had cleaned a man's hog for 'im, cut the hair off it and all that, and he'd give 'im a shoulder. He cut the shoulder off for my mother and she fried it and made some biscuits. With the biscuit we had somethin' to sop a little s'rup that he'd made. Then we went in and sat down in the livin' room to listen to the radio. The Lone Ranger was on. I listened to 'im for a little bit but got sleepy and turned it off and went in and layed down.

My brother come in early that night. I don't know where he'd come in from, but he'd come in early and he was havin' a good time at it. "Well," my dad said, "In the mornin', I want you two boys up early. We gonna go out in the field and we gonna load some watermelons up."

My brother told 'im, he said, "But I got a job in town I got to go to. I can't go out there and load watermelons."

My dad turned to me and said, "Ok. Well, you can come out there and help me load them watermelons."

I said, "All right. I can do that. I can do that."

Best Cabbage You Could Eat

Chapter 24

Well, I went out to the field and turned down Honeycutt Road and went on down 2-3 miles to the dippin' vat, and there was a mule. I opened the gate and went in there. I got a load of watermelons. The guy was goin' to La Coochie to sell 'em over there. And then whenever he'd leave La Coochie, he'd take some over to Mr. Cason and give 'im some millet. He'd trade 'im for watermelons. He said, "Now you can go with me or I'll let you out on Merritt Road up by Honeycutt, or I'll take you to Highway 48 and you can catch you a ride home."

I said, "Well, let me out at Honeycutt. I think there's more people on Highway 27 than they is on 48."

He said, "Ok." I got out and walked probably 'bout half a mile down there and saw this man in the cabbage patch. I knowed 'im. He said, "Hey, where you goin'?"

And I said "I'm goin' home to Okahumpka."

He said "Oh, ok. I'll tell you what. If you come over here and help me cut this cabbage that I'm gonna take it to the store in Leesburg, I'll take you to Okahumpka."

I thought, *Well, that beats walkin'.* So I went over there and took my pocket knife out. I kept it sharp and I cut cabbage, me and his daughter and 'im. He had 2 other kids, 3 other kids, but they was young so they warn't cuttin'. I come to the house and ate lunch with 'im; and by the way, we're still friends today. I ate lunch with 'im and we took and went back outside and I cut cabbage again with 'im 'til 'bout 2:00 or 3:00.

Well, he got some sacks and tied them sacks on the side of his car. He filled a trunk full. He filled the backseat with all of us in it so there was 2 in the front seat and 5 in the backseat and a bunch of cabbage. So we come on down the road, come to the house, and when I went to get out, he said, "Take one of them bags of cabbage with you."

And I said, "Yes, sir!"

He run on to the A&P Store and delivered them there. And I took my bunch of cabbage and I went in the house with it. My mama wanted to know where I got it. And I told her, "I got it from the man out there on the road."

She said, "Oh, I sure am glad to get it."

Well, she cooked the best cabbage you ever et. Whew Doggie! It was good! It'd jist melt in your mouth. I loved it. You could take some cabbage, two of them biscuits she makes, and that was jist perfect.

Well, nighttime's comin' and we went to bed at dark. We didn't have electricity and they wouldn't burn the kerosene 'cause it cost too much. It cost a nickel a gallon and they didn't want to burn all the kerosene up.

You Can't Beat Yankees

Chapter 25

So what we did then, the next mornin', I got up and I went over to Byron's house. He was fiddlin' around on the screen porch where he slept. We still had a little polecat smell to us. It warn't bad; you could stand it. He said, "Let's go to the creek."

I said, "Ok, we'll go down to the creek and go swimmin' in the spring." They's a little spring down there 'bout 200 yards; most people don't even know 'bout it. We knowed 'bout everythin' in every creek everywhere. So we started down and we saw this car in the orange grove.

Byron said, "Let's go check on it." So we walked down there out in the road.

He said, "That's a Yankee."

I said, "Yeah, it is."

He said, "They's stealin' oranges."

Said, "Yup."

Well, we knowed who the orange grove belonged to. It didn't belong to us. But Byron went up there and said, "Hey!" This woman had her dress pulled to hold oranges and she was puttin' oranges in it and dumpin' 'em back in the car. He was pickin' 'em and she was puttin' them in. Byron said, "Well, I see y'all is stealin' oranges."

They said, "Well, we gettin' a few to eat."

Byron said, "Look like 2 dollars worth to me."

"Oh, no, it ain't worth that," he said.

Byron said, "Well, you can either pay me or you can pay my dad or you can go to jail. I got your tag number and I'm gonna give it to 'im when I get back home if I don't get 2 dollars."

The man said, "Well, it ain't 2 dollars' worth."

Byron said, "Well, it ain't no difference if you stealin' 'em."

So the man dug in his pocket and he come up with two dollars and he handed it to Byron. And we started walkin' off. The guy said, "Can I get some more?"

And we said, "Get all you want."

We walked out on the old hog back road. Byron handed me a dollar and said, "Well, that's the easiest dollar we ever made."

We walked on down across to the bridge and went down on the east side of the Palatlakaha Creek, chucked our clothes and went swimmin' in the spring for 'bout an hour. Then we put our clothes back on and come back down the road and got down to the store. They was a feller down there who wanted to now if we'd like to help 'im move some watermelons. We said, "Yeah, we can go help 'im."

So we went out to the other side of Bridges Road, turned in there, went back toward Slot Machine Lake. And we loaded his watermelons up; he give us 2 dollars each. We'd done made 3 dollars that day! We was rich! Whew, we was rich!!

Income and the Straw Hat

Chapter 26

We was talkin 'bout what we was gonna do with that three dollars. So we thought all 'bout this thang and we said, "You know what? Uncle Will ain't got a straw hat. Let's hop the train tomorrow and go to town and buy 'im a straw hat."

He said, "Ok."

Byron had an old hat his daddy had give 'im and I had my old Stetson hat my daddy had give me, but Will didn't have a decent hat. So we hopped the train, got off at Leesburg, walked down the road and I said, "Well, where do you want to go get 'im a hat?"

Said, "The bargain store."

So we went down to the bargain store and we looked at hats. They was a straw hat there for a dollar and we bought it. And we bought 'im a red handkerchief. It was ten cents. Then we headed back.

We walked out to Highway 27, stuck our thumb up and caught a ride. The man at the dairy, he wouldn't pick us up. So we caught us another ride. The feller let us off in Okahumpka and we thanked 'im for it. We got off and we walked down the clay road toward Uncle Will's house. He was sittin' outside smokin' his pipe. Of course, he always layed it down and we'd get a drag off it. I don't know what he was smokin' in it but it didn't make no difference. It jist made smoke.

And we give 'im the straw hat and the bandanna.

The ole colored man cried. He said, "Boys, y'all worked all day long to get me this straw hat." We kind of laughed. And he said, "This red bandanna, I always wanted me one of 'em." Well, it felt good to us.

So I said, "Well, today's endin' and I think I better go home." So we walked back down the clay road. Byron went to his house and I walked across the field. Walked home. Supper was ready. Mama made a big pot of rabbit dumplin's. Whew Doggie! Them thangs is good. I ate me a big bowl of them rabbit dumplin's, washed my feet and washed my hands and my face. Went in and crawled into bed. It was all pleasant dreams 'til the next mornin'.

Next mornin' I got up, got my .22 and told my mama I was goin' over to the swamp to see if I could find some squirrels. Stopped by Byron's house and his mama said, "Byron's not here."

And I said, "Where's he at?"

She said, "He's gone to the front woods."

I said, "You mean Green Swamp?"

She said, "Yeah."

I said, "Oh, my goodness." So I decided I'd go over and lay in the tree house. I went by Uncle Will's but he warn't up yet. He musta been in the shine again. I went over to the tree house and climbed up in it and layed down on my bunk. I listened and looked and I thought, *This ain't no fun.*

I climbed down the tree house, went down across Uncle Will's. He was up and he wanted to know where Byron was at. I told 'im he'd gone to Front Woods.

"Oh, ok," he said. "Well, did you see anythin' down there?"

I said, "No. Nothin." I said, "But I ain't goin' in to Denham Swamp without 'im."

Said, "You don't need to be down there. And you shore don't need to be down there without someone bein' there with you."

I said, "I know. I'm goin' home now." So I started across the field.

Byron was back. They'd come in with a truck. Byron had been wadin' in that mud all day barefooted. He said that them moccasins was in that swamp, and I'm sure they was. He said, "But I'm not goin' back any more." He said, "My dad's truck rear end got banged up and we can't afford to have it fixed, so I'm not goin' back any more." It was an old truck.

I said, "You want to go to the swamp tomorrow?"

He said, "Yeah, we'll go to the swamp. Let's go down to Denham Swamp and see what's down there."

I said, "All right. I'll be here."

'Bout 7 o'clock the next mornin' I ate breakfast. I ate me three biskits and some s'rup and I had a little piece of fat back.

We eased over into Denham Swamp, climbed up in our tree. And he said, "You know, there's somethin' wrong with that snake. For some reason, that snake knows where we're at. We're gonna have to catch 'im without being here." He said, "We ought to build us a pen that he goes in and then we catch 'im. And then we get the snake man and bring 'im down here and get a thousand dollars."

I said, "I'm scared of that snake."

He said, "Well, think 'bout it."

We were layin' up there and we looked down and out walked that ole sow with them pigs that weighed 'bout 60 pounds apiece, and I said, "Byron, kill me one of them. My daddy wants one of them."

Byron took out his old .45-70 and I said, "Shoot 'im in the head," and he fired and that head exploded on that hog. He dropped to the ground. The minute he fired that big old snake was eyein' them pigs and he turned and went through the swamp. He was right on top of us and we didn't even know it!!

We went out there and got the pig, gutted it out. We lit a charcoal fire. They was some soldiers camped nearby. They come and ate that pig all in one night. They never ate a wild pig before, and they thought that was really somethin'!

One of them soldiers told me, "You ought to get you a better rifle than that .22." He said, I can't give you my M1, but you ought to get you a better rifle."

So we spent the day there. That night around dark, I took my bath 'cause I was muddy from one end to the other. My mama took the water and washed me down. I went in and went to bed and went to sleep. I slept good. I knowed that I had done somethin' good that day.

I got up the next mornin'. It was a Saturday mornin' and I thought, *Well, wonder what I'm gonna do today?*

My mama informed me that school was gonna start Monday mornin'. I said, "Uh-oh." I didn't want that. I didn't want to go to school.

I said, "I get my education over there in that swamp from Uncle Will. He teaches me thangs the school won't teach me. But I knowed I didn't have no choice 'cause when my mama decided somethin', all the rest of that stuff went by the wayside.

Settlin' the Score

Chapter 27

I didn't want to go to school. I wanted to catch that snake out in the woods. But I knowed my mama ain't gonna have that. We got there to school and we had a new teacher. We didn't like her. But we had to roll with the flow.

So we got in there and she told us what we was gonna do. We had 6 classes in one room; they was 4 or 5 in one, and 3 or 4 in another, and 5 or 6 in another. I think they was 30 all together, but I ain't sure 'bout that number. So she told us who she was and we told her who we was. I didn't think she was gonna put up with no nonsense.

Well, we went through the day and right behind the school we had a rope back there with a swing on it. We had a side swing with moss on it and we'd go back there and swing on it. They was a man behind the school who didn't like us swingin' there, so he sawed that limb off! That was the only limb we could have that thang on. And he had sawed it right off! We was very unhappy and there warn't nothin' we could do 'bout it.

So we went in and told our teacher we warn't happy 'bout it, and she said there ain't nothin' she could do. We had the play ground out in front of the buildin', and we had our clay, and we'd play marbles and play holes and knuckles. Sometimes them girls would take our marbles away.

We got to thinkin' 'bout that swing. It jist ain't right for someone to come in and tear our swing down. I mean, it ain't right!

So we went down to Bugg Spring and got ourselves a bamboo pole and a piece of wire. I went to bed in my clothes and slipped out the window that night, got the pole, and went over to his chicken pen with a piece of wire on the end with a loop on it. I'd tap that chicken and put it over his head and pull the thang really quick and his head would flop off, and he'd lay out on the ground. You always got the bottom chicken; you never did get the top. They was probably 'bout 10 ole hens and a rooster. I got 'em all!

Well, the next mornin' we went to school, but lo and behold, here come the guy with a stick. He was gonna beat every single one of them boys in there 'til he found out who killed his chickens.

Well, the teacher told 'im to get out. He informed her he warn't gonna get out. She got the broom out of the closet and hit 'im upside the head with that broom. He took off out the door and he was shakin' his stick sayin', "I'll get you, I'll get you!"

Well, the next day he was movin' his stuff out 'cause the school board had done come and moved 'im out. I think that teacher done called the school board and they called 'im out.

We was sittin' in the class in there that was heated with a wood heater. The boys would have to go outside and get the wood for the heater and put it in it.

My brother started the fire every mornin'. He was the janitor of the school whenever he was in the 7th or 8th grade in Leesburg. He cleaned it up every afternoon and got five dollars a month from the county.

We got in there and they talked 'bout playground equipment. They said they was gonna get us a swing set. We got all excited 'bout that. Then they decided they warn't goin' to get us a swing set; so we warn't excited 'bout that.We was jist layin' back there on the limb, but we didn't have another limb we could put our swing on, so knowed we warn't goin' to get a swing set.

Then we all made us rubber band guns. We got red rubber to make them. We'd cut it around and put a thang on it and put a clothespin on the back and we had a pistol that would shoot rubber bands. It wouldn't shoot 'em very far, but it'd shoot far enough to hit you. And we played rubber bands for 'bout an hour.

What To Do
'bout Mean Bulldogs

Chapter 28

We walked down to the store after we got out of school. There was a sidewalk, the only sidewalk in Okahumpka was between the school and our big old house. The owner was a school teacher at one time in Okahumpka, and her husband worked at the depot. So they was purty well off. They had the finer thangs in life. But she had an old white bulldog and every time you'd go past, that ole white bulldog'd come out and he'd nip at your heels like he was gonna bite you.

I said, "Byron, don't y'all have a pistol?"

He said, "Yeah, we got a .32 lemon squeezer."

I said, "What's a lemon squeezer?"

He said, "You gotta squeeze the handle before you can pull the trigger."

I said, "If you would bring that thang to school, I'll kill that white bulldog."

He said, "Well, I'll sure bring it. I'll load it up."

I tell 'im, "Ok."

That day he rode his bike to school. I didn't have one, so he would come and tow me on this bicycle. We started out and here come that ole white bulldog. He was a growlin' and I was shootin' at 'im and "she" was watchin' us. Them bullets was ricochetin' off the road and that dog was scratchin' and tryin' to get away. But I finally ran out of shells. We went on down to the store and Byron dropped me off at the depot before he went on home. He took the pistol with 'im.

He said, "My daddy'd probably beat my behind if he knowed I was takin' off with this-here pistol."

I warn't thinkin' 'bout it much, but 'bout dark "she" rolls up in that old '36 Buick. I thought, *Hmmm, well, I'm fixin' to get it.* So I went around the house where the hogs had little pigs. I thought I didn't need to be in the yard whenever my daddy comes in. Well, he come in at jist dark and she lit in on 'im.

She said, "Your boy tried to kill my bulldog."

He yelled for me and I knowed I had to go.

He said, "Did you try to kill her bulldog?"

And I said, "Yes, sir, I did." I said, "Every time we try to go down there that bulldog tries to bite us and we're tired of it."

He said, "Well, I'll tell you what you do. The next time you go down there, don't take no pistol to shoot no bulldog. Take that shotgun and two buckshot shells and kill that dog."

Then he turned to her and he said, "Is there anythin' else you want to talk to me 'bout?"

She got in that ole '36 Buick, put it in reverse, backed up and backed square into a big ole oak tree. It had one of them suitcases on the back and it smashed it in and busted the glass right out. She put it in low gear and sprung off down through the dirt road.

We was standin' there watchin' and my daddy said, "I think she's mad, boy. Stay away from her."

And that was all that was ever said.

Makin' Mulberry Wine

Chapter 29

Come Saturday mornin' we walked over to Uncle Will's. It was kinda rainin', so we didn't think we'd want to go over into the swamp. We decided we'd make us a gallon of mulberry wine. But we didn't know exactly how to do it. We'd tried it before and failed. So we was goin' to go ask Uncle Will how to make mulberry wine, 'cause we knowed he could tell us. He'd probably drunk enough of it.

So we went over to Uncle Will and said, "We wanna make us some mulberry wine. How do we make it?"

He said, "Whew Doggie! Whenever you get it made I want some of it."

We said, "Ok. How do you make it?"

He said, "Well, you got to have some yeast. I got some of that. You got to have sugar. I got some of that. And then you got to pick lots of mulberries."

We said, "There's lots of them on that-there tree over there. If we don't get them the birds is goin' to."

He said, "Now, this is the way you make mulberry wine. You pick 'bout 1 of them foot tubs full of mulberries, and then you get someone in there and squish all them mulberries up with your feet."

I said, "Huh?"

"Well, then, whenever you get them all squished, you take that flour sack and put the berries in that jug. You put 'em in between them two boards that you use to get the grease out of cracklin's. You know, 1 of them 2 boards together with the hinge on it?"

We said, "Yeah, we know 'em boards; we got one of 'em."

"Then you take and put it in this gallon jug with the sugar and the yeast and you shake it up real good.

Than you take and wire that inner tube on so it don't leak. If it leaks, then it won't make wine. And then, whenever that thang gets to shakin' and blowin' that inner tube up—it'll take a few days to blow it up. Then you take and wait 'til it all leaks down and the inner tube jist falls over. Then you get yourself a croker sack and sift all the bad stuff out of it and pour what you got back in the jug. You got some finger-lickin' good wine!"

So we said, "We got it down pat!" We took the yeast and the sugar he had. He knowed he was goin' to get it back, and we went to Byron's house. It was startin' to rain once again, but that didn't make no difference. We'd been wet before. We got us a foot tub and we picked us a bucket of mulberries. It takes a while.

One thang you don't do on a mulberry; you don't blow on 'em 'cause whenever you do all the bugs come to the top and you see 'em. You jist go ahead and eat 'em without blowin' on them. If you blow on 'em, you don't want to eat them bugs and everythin'.

We picked for 'bout 2 or 3 hours and there was Byron's sister. She was sittin' there watchin'. She wanted to know what we was doin'. We told her we was goin' to make us some mulberry wine.

She said, "Ok."

We got that foot tub with all we could put in it and was tryin' to figure out who was goin' to get into that foot tub and smash them berries.

Byron said, "You gonna get in there?"

I said, "I don't wanna get in there." Betty Jean didn't want to get in there either.

And then we looked and there come Byron's younger brother. Byron broke off a piece of that ole Black Cow candy and handed it to 'im. He said, "Larry, how 'bout smashin' them mulberries for me?"

He said, "I can do that." He was 'bout 4 years old, maybe 5. He'd been down in the cow pasture too. Ain't telling what he stepped in, but that don't matter either. Uncle Will gonna drink it. So he got in there and he smashed them mulberries. He said it was fun. He said, "I feel 'em between my toes."

Ain't no tellin' what had been through them toes. We made 'im wash is feet before he got in there. Well, he mashed 'em for 'bout an hour. It got purty soupy and it turned his legs blue 'bout up to his knees.

We told 'im, "Ok, you can get out."

So he got out and went over there where the water was at. Guess what! He couldn't wash all them berries off 'im. He had 'bout his knees down covered in blueberry juice. But that was alright. It would wear off eventually. So then we got a feed sack. We sifted it through and put it in a tin. Then we got that squeezin' thang that you squeeze hog chitlins to get the grease out of the skins – cracklin' is what they called it. And we squeezed 'em out best we could.

The juice was purty. It was. It was purty and I'd drink that. We had probably 'bout a jug full. We got that ole red inner tube and we got us some wire, and we wired it on the top. Where the fingers go on the jug, we wired it there and on the top. We said, "There ain't no way it can leak." And we took a pair of pliers and made it tight. We took it and set it in the barn, right in the back corner where nothin' would bust the jar.

Then Byron's mama come out. And I'll tell you right now, I think she was jist a little bit mad!! She jumped on 'im and told 'im, "You gonna scrub every bit of that off'n Larry's legs!"

There ain't no way to scrub it off. That thang's done. I mean, I'll tell you, it was done. He was blue.

I said, "I guess he'll jist have to wear it off."

I didn't think that was the wrong thang to tell her, but she was jist fit to be tied.

Now, we'd watch this jug every day. All at once we looked in there and it was bubblin'. I told Byron, I said, "It's a-rottin' in there."

He said, "Sure looks like it. Wonder if it'll be fit to drink?"

"I don't know."

Then we looked in 'bout 2 weeks later. That rubber done blew up like a balloon. And we knowed it was a makin' wine. A couple more weeks and the rubber fell over, jist like Uncle Will said it would.

We went and seen Uncle Will and he said, "Boys, whenever the rubber's gone over, that means it's quit makin' wine, and you need to do somethin' with it, else it'll turn to vinegar."

I told 'im, "Ok."

So we went back and we strained it through a croker sack. We took and got that thang to get them hog skins with. And then we got that sack and we squeezed all we could squeeze out of it. We put it in a jug and then we said, "You know what? We need to taste this."

So we got us a little bit in a food jar. I didn't like it. It didn't taste good to me at all. I thought it'd taste good like pink soda water or somethin' like that. But it didn't. So we took that jug and we went over to Uncle Will's.

Said, "Uncle Will, we got this wine made."

He said, "Have you-all tasted it?"

I said, "I did and I don't like it."

So he poured 'im out some in the glass. He sloshed some around in his mouth and said, "It ain't bad boys. It ain't bad wine at all. It tastes like you've got a little somethin' missin', but it ain't bad."

Byron, he got some there and he tasted it, and he said he didn't like it either. So we started back over to Byron's house. We said, "You know what? We'll put in some of that shine and he'll like it."

We got to the spring and we crossed it on that cable that's hand-over-hand. That's a hard crossin 'cause that ole cable's got a bunch of little wires stuck up and I was barefooted. We walked across that thang.

Over there where the man had his 'shine bottles hid up there beneath the stump. We put a quarter in the can and got us a bottle of shine. Then we carried it back across and went back to Uncle Will's. We didn't' let 'im see us. We poured a pint of that shine in it and shook that jug up good.

Well, the next day was Sunday. We went to church. Got out of the church 'bout 1 o'clock and went by Uncle Will's. We got a drag off his pipe. We knowed he woulda been smokin'. We looked at 'im and his eyes was bloodshot. He said, "Boys, that wine y'all made."

We said, "What do you mean?"

He said, "Well, I got me a glass of it and I drank that whole glass. It sure tastes good now! The next thang I 'member, I was layin' in the yard and I layed out there all night. I feel like I been run over by that freight train. But I'm gonna tell you somethin'. Ya'll make a good jug of wine!"

So we paddy-padded back across the field to Byron's house and went to church that night. Then we went home to bed.

Tomorrow's another day.

Back to The Swamp

Chapter 30

I got up early and went to Byron's house. Byron's house is between me and the swamp and that's the reason why I'm always goin' over there.

Byron's sister had a friend from Leesburg come out to spend the night with her Sunday night. They wanted to go down and get in that tree house we'd built and watch the varmints. So we said, "Alright."

So we went to Uncle Will's. He was sittin' outside on his porch hummin' a song. I don't know what it was. We waved at 'im and went on.

I told Byron to carry his rifle. I didn't have mine with me. So he had his. He picked up two shells and said that would be enough. So we went over there and climbed up in the tree. We turned our mattresses sideways so everybody'd have somethin' to lay on. And we watched a possum come down with a bunch of little possums. Saw a black snake come through. He was gettin' somethin' for supper after lunch, I guess. And then we heared a noise in the bushes. Byron said, "Here come that ole boar hog again." But it warn't a boar hog!

It crawled right out where we could see it. It was 'bout 30 yards from us. The sweat poured off me like it was rainin'. I looked at Byron; he leveled that rifle up and I thought that snake's head was a gonna fly.

He pulled the trigger and the gun jist snapped. He pulled the back part of that gun to reset the thang and it snapped again. He undid it, went to put another shell in and the snake turned and went in the woods. He took the ole bullet out and looked at it. It was an ole bullet; copper, probably made it 60 years ago, and he throwed it out there in the woods. We sat there a minute breathin' hard. All of a sudden that shell went, "POP!" It didn't hardly make any noise at all. The powder in it had probably been wet from time. Only reason that snake warn't dead is that bullet didn't go off. He'd a-blowed that snake's head off better than anythin'.

I was sweatin'. I was sweatin' all over. I jist knowed that that snake was dead. Betty Jean and her friend from Leesburg, they was sittin' there, and they wanted to know what was wrong with us. We said, "We missed that snake again. That's three times that we made a mistake and that snake got away."

Byron said, "Did you see that snake look at us there up in that tree? He knows we're up there in that tree. He knows whenever we're up there, and he knows whenever he's safe and we're not. I think that he's after us instead of us after 'im, but we're gonna get that snake, 'cause he's worth a hundred dollars, and we never had a hundred dollars before. So we gonna get 'im."

Well, we climbed down out of the tree and went back by Uncle Will's. He was sittin' there and we got us a drag off his pipe. We told 'im what had happened and he said, "Boys! Stay away from that swamp. There ain't nothin' but trouble down there; you don't know what you can get into down there."

We said, "Well, we got to kill that snake."

He said, "Well, you ain't killed 'im so far and ain't nobody else either. That snake's smarter than ya'll."

So we left Uncle Will and walked back across the field there. We walked by the cow pen where there might be maybe two or three people swingin' on the swing. But jist 'bout everybody was down there swingin' on it.

I said, "Well, I've had 'bout all I can stand for today. I'm goin' home." I walked across the field, and I was very disappointed. We had lost our hundred dollars that day. It was such a perfect shot and Byron wouldn't have missed. He was too good to miss. But tomorrow's another day and we'll jist have to try again.

I went home and washed my feet, washed my hands and washed

my face, and went to bed. All night long I dreamed 'bout that-there snake. He was in the tree with us. He was out of the tree. He was on the ground; he was in the ground. Everythin' 'bout it, I dreamed 'bout it.

The War

Chapter 31

So, come Monday mornin' we went to school. Nothin' excitin' happened at school that day. We all jist had recess, ate lunch, studied books and all 'bout the War of 1812. I didn't care nothin 'bout the War of 1812. I didn't care much 'bout the First World War, never mind the War of 1812.

So, Byron and me, we go fishin' that afternoon up to Shaw Pond. The church was gonna have a fish fry, so we told 'em we could go catch enough fish for it. Out at the pond there's a hole 'bout as big as a washtub and every time we'd throw our line in there, we'd catch a bass. We got us a pole with our knives and wire, and we tied that wire to them fish, and we was carryin' them down the road.

A man stopped and picked us up. We layed our fish in the back of his truck. He said, "Boys, we're in trouble."

We said, "What's wrong?"

He said, "Well, Pearl Harbor jist got bombed."

We said, "Where's Pearl Harbor?"

And he told us it was out in the Pacific Ocean. He said, "We're at war with Japan."

We went to Byron's house and cleaned the fish and then we went to church. We smelled like fish but nobody paid no attention. We'd caught enough fish for them to have a fish fry.

After church, we walked down by the beer joint. It was open and the Victrola in there was playin'. They all gathered there. They was 'bout 4 of 'em that was old enough to go to the army. They all loaded up in the car. Somebody got in the car with them and they went to Jacksonville.

One of the 4 didn't come back from the war. We had quite a few people that went off to war. My brother did; my cousin did. They jist left. Some come back but some didn't.

Whenever stuff got scarce, like sugar and meat, you got coupons. And the coupons bought shoes too. You could get 2 pair of shoes a year. I didn't care nothin' 'bout shoes, so my brother got 'em. Gasoline was rationed. They was search lights all over Okahumpka. But I figured the Germans wouldn't attack Florida. They probably did; we jist didn't know 'bout it.

The Turkey Shoot

Chapter 32

We still had a problem. We had that snake over yonder in them woods. We went down and bought Byron a box of them .45-70s; there was 'bout 20 of them in a box and I give 'im a box, so that gave 'im 40 shells. We figured that'd be enough for 'im to kill anythin' in them woods.

We'd go down and shoot the squirrels and we'd divide them up. We trapped a quail. We did everythin' that you could think of. We worked in the boxcars. It warn't no trouble to get a job. They'd hire almost anybody. All you had to do was work.

So we decided 1 afternoon after school that we would go back over by the creek. There was a bass on a bed. Big ole bass. We made us a snatch hook. Went over there, eased that line down in there and snatched 'im up on it. I mean the water boiled and twisted and turned and everythin' else. We pulled it up and it was an old mudfish! I thought, *Huh! That warn't no mudfish we saw before*. But I guess that's what it was. So we throwed 'im up on the bank and let the coons eat 'im.

We went to school the next Monday and the minute we got there the teacher told us that they may close down the Okahumpka School. We didn't want them to do that. We wanted to go to school there. Finally they decided to let us stay.

I went down to Byron's house on Saturday mornin' and then we went down to the store. We got us a can of Prince Albert. We'd done run out of it.

Well, there's a sign there in the window of the store, right next to the sign that posted your name if you didn't pay your bill. This new sign said, "Turkey Shoot – 10 o'clock Saturday Mornin' – Bring Your Gun - Bring Your Ammunition - You'll be Shooting at Live Turkeys"

I turned to Byron, I said, "Byron, we got 2 dollars. We can get us a turkey for your mama and 1 for my mama."

So Byron went back home and got his rifle and four bullets. He said, "That's all we need." Then we come back down at 10 o'clock. There was people shootin', and ole Bill was there. He shot 3 times. I saw 'im hit the log. So Byron said he wanted to shoot. He layed on the ground and rested his rifle on the log, and the man said, "Go right ahead."

But that turkey would lift his head up and when you pulled the trigger he'd duck. There'd been 'bout 25 to 30 people who shot at it. The man was makin' money, a dollar for every shot. He'd made 'bout 30 dollars off that 1 turkey.

Unbeknownst to the seller, I told Byron, I said, "Now when you get ready, I'll gobble with this mouthpiece I got, a turkey call, and he'll stick his head up and you can blow it off."

He said, "Ok. You got it."

Well, I was standin' there and he said, "Now!" And I gobbled on that turkey call and that turkey stuck his head up, and he shot if off. Whew Doggie! That fella was unhappy. He was unhappy! Unhappy! We'd done shot his turkey and everybody around there was laughin' 'bout it. I don't think he'd got half as mad if there warn't the laughin'. But they was laughin'.

He said, "No, you're not gonna get that turkey!" The fellas down there argued with 'im so much that he finally agreed to let us have it. But he said, "No more turkey calls."

We said, "Ok". Well, they shot another round, probably been 25 -30 people shot. Ole Bill had shot 'bout 5 times, and he got nothin'.

Byron paid his dollar and the man said, "No turkey call. No turkey call."

We said, "Ok, no turkey call." Byron layed down there in the position. Me and 'im hunted down in them woods enough to know how to do thangs. He hollered, "Now!" and that old turkey stuck his head up and he busted it off. That fella got up off the ground and said, "I said no turkey calls."

I said, "Hey, look he didn't use no turkey call. He jist said, "Now." That's when he was gonna shoot." So I said, "You gonna give that boy them turkeys."

So I done picked the feathers almost all of them off the one I had over there, and I was pickin' the ones off of Byron's. We saved them long feathers to make our headdress like them Injuns. That helps us to not be seen in the woods.

Well, Larry wanted one. We made ours out of turkey feathers but we didn't have no more. A buzzard had been kilt on Highway 27 so we got them black feathers and made 'im a headdress. If his mama had knowed what we had done, she would have beat us both. So when we got some feathers that come from a hawk we changed 'em. It looked real good.

Well, the man come up to us and said, "You're purty good with that rifle. Have you ever drove a nail?"

Nail Drivin'

Chapter 33

"Oh yeah," he said, "I'll drive a nail."

So the man got a 16-penny nail and put it up there, but Byron said, "I can't see it." It was 'bout 50 yards away.

Said, "If you put some white paint on the end of it so I can see it, then I can drive it."

The man said, "You got it, boy."

And he went down and got some paint somewhere and daubed some on the end of that nail. Byron layed down there and got in the position and "POW!" that nail was gone. Well, the fella, he was bettin' 20 dollars. He said that Byron had broke the nail off; he didn't drive it. So they got a hatchet and they chopped in there and saw that he did drive it. He told Byron, "Well, can you shoot another one?"

And Byron said, "I only got 1 more shell and I don't want to get rid of it, cause we got a snake in the woods we tryin' to kill."

"Well, I'm gonna tell you what," he said. "I'm gonna get you some more shells. B.D. Harrison's got them."

So we said, "Ok," and we went into town. I rode in with 'im and Bryon stayed there to finish pickin' all the feathers off the turkeys. We went to B.D. Harrison, and he bought two boxes. I don't remember how much they cost but they was expensive. Them was big ole bullets.

We come back and they done drove 5 nails in that log. The fella was bettin' with 'em, but they warn't white on the heads. So he said, "Go down there and paint them nails white." So they walked down there, looked at 'em, called everybody down there and said, "I want you to look what this fella's tryin' to do. Them nails is crooked. You can't drive them thangs in with a hammer!"

"Oh yeah, you could. Here's a hammer. Drive 1 in." He hit at 1 and it bent over.

He said, "Now we put straight nails in; then we'll get down to some serious bettin.'" I drove five nails in and painted 'em white.

He said, "Now, would you like to bet a hundred dollars?"

One said, "Sure."

One fella standin' there said, "There ain't no way he can drive that nail in again. That was jist luck the first time."

He said, "You got a hundred dollars?"

"Yeah, I got a hundred dollars."

"So put your money where your mouth is."

He said, "All right. I'll bet."

His brother said, "All right. I'll bet you a hundred dollars too."

Byron layed down there in the position and said, "POW!" And that nail went, "Poof."

They said that he missed it. But he hit the side of it and the nail flew in. So we went down there with a hatchet and chopped it down 'bout half an inch, quarter of an inch, come to the lid and then come to the head of the nail.

He said, "Huh!" You'd better pay up or else you'd better suffer the consequences." So they paid up.

We won two hundred dollars off that man, well, actually three. And he said, "Does anybody else want to bet a hundred dollars?"

"No."

"Does anybody want to bet twenty dollars?"

"No."

He said, "Here boy, here's twenty dollars. Drive another one." Byron layed there and put another bullet in. "POW!" He drove another in right up to the head.

He said, "Boy, you good. Where'd you learn to shoot like that?"

Byron said, "I was born shootin'."

He said, "You're good. You're better than most. Someday I might come and get you and we'll go up there in the old National Forest on that shoot-off they have up there, and we'll make a little money there."

He started to leave and handed me ten dollars and said, "Here, here's your ten dollars." I was glad to get it.

Byron could give me half the twenty, but I didn't expect 'im to do it. Byron gathered up the empty hulls. A man over in Eustis, if we could get somebody to take us over there, would reload them for us. But he didn't like to use 'im, 'cause he never knowed where the bullet was goin' to go on the reloads.

We walked on back down the clay roads. I walked home and gave my mama the turkey, cut the guts out and cleaned the gizzard, cut the liver off, cut the heart out, took the rest of the insides and threwed it in the hog's pen. The hogs ate it.

She baked the turkey. It was a really good turkey. I didn't pick all the pin feathers out but she went in and picked 'em all out before she cooked it. We had it for Sunday dinner. Had a turkey and cherry pie, mashed taters, sweet taters, always had sweet taters; then she baked some of her homemade biskits. Whew! Were they good. She had 1 of them round thangs she put jelly in – jelly in the middle of it, and Whew Doggie! My brother, he'd eat a pile of them thangs!

Buildin' a Raft

Chapter 34

Friday afternoon and we decided we was gonna build us a raft. So we went down to the pasture behind this house to get us a bunch of green persimmons; took our clothes off and waded out in that pond. Here come two black women. They was school teachers. They didn't like what we was doin'. They told us to get out of that pond and get our clothes on. I went to the bank. She grabbed her a switch and hit my behind with it and told me to get my clothes on. She didn't want to catch us out there again with no clothes on.

After they left I told Byron, I said, "You know, I think that woman was mad at us. Do you?"

He said, "Yes, she was mad at us."

So we went home, but we was still gonna build us a raft.

We left our shoes out there 'cause we didn't want to get 'em wet. We got out there and built that raft and drug it out to 'bout waist deep and turned it loose. It sunk to the bottom. I don't mean slow-like. It jist sunk to the bottom. We figured 'cause it was a tree it didn't float. So we thought, *Uncle Will can tell us how to build a raft.*

So we went to Uncle Will's. He was sittin' out back under that old tin shed playin' with 1 of them goats. He fed 'em and they was fat and doin' good. We said, "Uncle Will, we want to build us a raft to float down

Bugg Spring."

He said, "Well, boys, I'll tell you how to build it. You go down there to Bugg Spring and you get that big bamboo. You cut them limbs off it, but don't throw 'em away. You throw all them leaves off them limbs and save 'em. They be 'bout 15 feet long. You get 'bout a dozen of 'em and you wire them thangs together. I got some wire in the back."

So we got us a thick roll of bamboo. Byron got in front and I got in the back and we carried that thang all the way down to Bugg Spring. We hauled the bamboo down and we sawed the ends off. And we left that lumber in down there so we could turn it back over and it wouldn't drag in the water. Then we layed the limbs on that. Since they were hollow, they'd float. Then we went on the other side of Bugg Spring and got the 1-inch bamboo. And we got 'bout thirty of 'em. And we cut them limbs off down there.

We started Saturday mornin' 'bout 9 o'clock and worked until late afternoon, so we drug it out there in the woods where nobody'd find it. And we said, "Next week we're goin' on a voyage!"

We had us some pushpoles we got off in the forest and we thought what we'd do is tie somethin' on the bottom where it wouldn't go in the mud. And we knowed we had to paddle it over to Helena Run. Saturday mornin', beautiful day, not hardly no wind, and we pushed that thang off of Bugg Spring. It floated! And we went and got on it. We'd made us a rudder on the back and stuck it down in that bamboo. The rudder warn't very long; it was 'bout 10 inches long. That was a mistake! But that warn't the first mistake we'd made.

We paddled that thang over there to Bugg Spring Run, and we was a driftin' along. We was goin' to be Tom Sawyer and Huckleberry Finn. But we warn't. So we poled the thang down past Sumter Landing, passed on down; the curves was hard to make, but we got down to Helena Run. We was tryin' to decide whether to go to Lake Denham or Lake Harris, but I said, "Let's go to Leesburg." I never been to Leesburg on the water. Well, we pushed it out along there. We met a boat and we had to get over to the side. He wanted to know what kind of contraption we thought we had. He wanted us to get off so he could get through and he gave us some choice words.

I said, "Byron, hit 'im over the head with that pushpole you got." But the man got out of the way; he didn't know whether we would do it or not.

So we poled it on down underneath the bridge. People was fishin' down there and they laughed 'bout us. We went on down there and we got on to Lake Harris. We got off a bit and then poled out into Lake Harris. We was doin' purty good. We was off the edge a little bit. We had to keep in mind the grass, 'cause the grass would slow us down.

We poled down to Lake Harris. Got to this open water, sort of a cove in there, and it flowed through there and to this island. They called it Corley Island. The water flowed through there and the wind was high. High! It caught the raft, went over it, turned the thang sideways and we was swimmin' in the middle of the lake! So standin' up, we couldn't do nothin' with it. The rudder part had caught the wind. A boat come by and we waved at 'im but he thought we was jist wavin' to be wavin'. We was wavin' 'cause we wanted 'im to pick us up. But he didn't. He jist waved back and went on.

Well, we got the raft back up and we could see where the cut-through was to Little Lake Harris and we was headed that direction. We knowed where that was. That was Howey. We said, "Well, if we go to Howey, then the old wooden bridge is over there. We can get on the wooden bridge and walk our way home." It's not too bad walkin' that far, but we'd done got farther than we should have and it was 'bout 3 o'clock.

So we went on past. The wind carried us in jist a little bit. We was purty well in there on the land and we tried to pole it but we couldn't. We went past 2 or 3 places that we knowed. There warn't nobody wavin' at us. We would've waved back if there had been. We'd wave our underwear at them if we'd thought they'd come out there and get us.

We didn't know where we was gonna wind up. I asked Byron if we went far enough that way would we get to Lake Eustis. But he didn't know. We come on down and the wind caught us and took us to Lake Harris. It put us right up there 'bout the mile where Lake Harris starts, and there was a house there. Well, we got the best of that thang, and we poled it in to this dock. We pulled it up on the bank and started to leave. A guy come out and informed us to come back and get that mess that we had. Well, we didn't want that mess. We'd done got farther than we needed to be as it was. So we run through the orange grove.

We run through it and come out on the highway. We wound up at

Catfish Creek at Echo Glen and went through there. We knowed we didn't want to get on the highway, 'cause that man might come by. We warn't too sure he wouldn't have one of 'em fellas with a badge with 'im, and we didn't need no fella with a badge.

So we come right up to the hammock, crossed over on the railroad track, walked the railroad tracks on down across Palatlakaha Creek. Then we crossed through there. We walked on the dirt road that ran by it. That got us down to Highway 27. It was 'bout 4 or 5 o'clock. I told Byron, I said, "Boy, what an adventure. I wish we could have made it to Leesburg."

If we hadn't got caught up in that cove up there where the wind caught us, we'd have made it to Leesburg. We could've walked home and gone down 27 to catch a ride.

Well, that ended this journey of our raftin'. We never did build another raft like that. We thought 'bout it though.

We did built 1 on the creek years later.

Fishin' Trip

Chapter 35

We went to school the next week and we decided we was goin' back over there. It'd been rainin' a lot and that swamp over there was rained on. We were tryin' to stay out of it 'cause it was so wet. But a man from out of his house come over to us and asked if we'd like to go fishin'.

He said, "Boys, I'll tell you how I do it. You go fishin' with me and I'll buy all the bait and I'll get the fishin' stuff and you get to keep 1 fish. You can keep 1 of them 5 or 10 pound fish. That'll be enough for y'all to have to eat."

I said, "You'll really give us 1 of them 5 or 10 pound fish?"

He said, "Yeah. And I'll pick y'all up on Saturday mornin' 'bout 5 o'clock."

We said, "Ok, we'll be ready."

So I went and told Byron to be ready at 5 o'clock and we'd meet 'im down at the store.

He told us he'd fix lunch for us too, a sandwich and somethin' to drink." He said, "Y'all will have a good time fishin'."

So we told 'im, "Ok, we'll go."

So Saturday mornin' bright and early we was down at the store 'bout 4:30. He come down in his truck and we had our hats on. I had a long sleeved shirt 'cause I burn so bad.

I had on a pair of gloves too; they was worn out, but they'd keep the sun off my hands. And I had my shoes on. Byron didn't have his shoes. He didn't burn like I did, so he had on a short-sleeve shirt; but he had his hat on.

We started off in Homosassa and went to Hell's Gate, which was down there. That guy knowed how to run that boat. That-there boat had a motor on it and it chugged along. We got there fast. Then we went out there and went past the bird roost. We kept goin' and goin' and goin' and every once in a while he'd stop and take a lead weight out. He'd throw that lead weight out and it'd hit the bottom. Whenever it hit the bottom, he'd pull it up and he'd look at it. I asked 'im, I said, "What you doin'?"

And he said, "I'm checkin' for rocks."

"For rocks? What are you goin' to do with them rocks?"

"That's where the fish is at," he said.

So we kept goin' a little bit and finally he said, "This is the spot."

He put out his anchor. We drifted back and he put 2 anchors out the back. He said, "Ok, boys, get your bait out and I'm gonna tell you how to do it. You put your bait on the hook and you drop it over 'til it hits the bottom. Then bring it up 'bout a foot. You let it sit there a minute; then you drop it down again and bring it up."

We said, "Ok, we got it."

I seen Byron over there; he let it down and brought it up. I could see that his pole had bent down, and I thought he had caught the bottom. Well, when he brought that ole grouper up, he weighed 'bout twenty pounds. We put it in the ice chest. We caught fish, they bit and he caught them and put 'em in that ice chest. He'd throw ice on top of 'em and we caught five or ten fish, then a bunch of young little grouper; and then he said, "Well, it's time to move."

We took the anchors up and we moved down 'bout 200 yards where he found another rock bed. And we did the same thang over again. We had a boatload of fish. So he said, "Well, it's 'bout 3 o'clock; time to go."

So, we pulled the anchors up, cranked the boat and we come back to Okahumpka. He gave us both a big ole grouper and some others. My dad had to gut it. It was 'bout 15-18 lbs. He liked fish and me too. So my mama fried them fresh fish up and she put the rest of 'em in lard. She tied a string around 'em and then pushed 'em in the lard bucket so they'd keep. We didn't have a 'frigerator.

And then, whenever she wanted to cook them, she'd pull 1 of 'em up and brush most of the lard off before cookin'. They was so good. They was better than most fish. That was a really good fishin' trip.

Red, some years later, as a teenager, and a big bass he caught.

Woods Fire

Chapter 36

Sunday mornin' a deputy come to the house. I thought. *What have we done now? That man over there in Howey done turned us in?*

He said, "Boys, y'all burn the woods off."

I said, "When?"

He said, "Saturday."

I said, "We didn't burn the woods off."

He said, "Oh, yes you did. Bill said you did."

Byron said, "I knowed we should have shot 'im."

I said, "We didn't do it."

He said, "Well, let's go over here in the grove."

We went to the grove and Bill had set them woods on fire where our tree house to lay down is. He'd burned all up around Hwy 27 where Helena Run traveled, jumped Helena Run and burned north. It burned in there all around the sawmill. They got it and put it out, and it didn't burn up no houses. Then they's another house over there on the clay road. They fought the fire to keep it off of it. It burned on down and it burned the city dump. I mean, it burnt that dump up! It burnt for 'bout a week and finally the fire department went down and tried to put it out.

It burnt less toward Okahumpka, but it didn't burn that far. It went down the canal over there and the wind changed and blew it back off of it. Then a big rain come and put the fire out. But it had burned all the rest of that sawgrass in there. It had burned where the ole burnt-out stumps was, but it hadn't got our house down there that we built. So he said, "Bill said y'all set this fire and he saw you do it."

"Well, we didn't set no fire. We was out fishin' with a man."

"Well," he said, "Let's go talk to the man who you went out with to go fishin." We told 'im he picked us up 'bout 4:30 or 5:00 and we went to Homosassa. We fished over there and he brought us home 'bout 5 o'clock. And we was down at the store; Bill was down there and he said, "Yeah, I saw them. I saw them set it."

One of them grove workers was there that we knowed, and he come up and he said, "Bill's lyin'. Bill set the fire. I saw 'im do it. He come down there in that old cut-up truck and he got out and poured diesel fuel on the ground, and then he set it on fire and left."

So we all went down to the hammock, and sure enough, there was Bill's tracks; there was two big ole tire tracks. So he wrote Bill a ticket, and he warn't happy 'bout that.

We warn't happy 'bout that either, but we was jist happy we warn't goin' to jail. So they took Bill to court and we got up before the judge. The judge asked us point blank, he said, "Boys, did ya'll set that hammock on fire down there?"

We said, "No, sir. We didn't set it."

"You didn't set it?"

"No, sir. We didn't set it." Said, "We was fishin' in Homosassa."

He said, "Well, Bill says you all the time down there."

Said, "Yeah he says that, but we didn't set it. We don't know who set it."

Well, the deputy got up. I think his name was Leroy, but I'm not sure. He said, "Your honor, them boys didn't set it. Bill set it and I got an eye witness to it."

Bill's mouth fell to the ground. He knowed he had been had. Said, "This man been workin' in the grove and he saw Bill come down in his truck. He set the fire. And it burnt everythin'. It didn't burn no houses, but it burned 'bout everythin' up."

Judge said, "Well, what do you got to say 'bout that, Bill?"

Bill said, "Well, maybe it warn't them."

Judge said, "You're the one who set this fire. And I'm gonna fine you 250 dollars. And I'm gonna give you a 90-day suspended sentence. If I hear of any more trouble out of you, or you bother these boys any more, you gonna go to jail and serve that 90 days. Do you understand what I'm sayin'?"

"Yes, sir."

"Ok, case dismissed."

He said "Boys, what are you doin' down there in that big ole swamp anyways?"

We said, "We tryin' to kill that big snake."

He said, "There's a big snake in there?"

We said, "Yes, sir. It's a rattlesnake and that thang is thirty feet long."

He said, "Aw, there ain't no thirty-foot long rattlesnakes."

We said, "Yes sir, there is. We seen 'im three or four times."

He said, "Well, you boys be careful. I'm glad that it ain't no problem."

We said, "Well, it's not no problem. We jist had a good day of fishin'."

He said, "Ok, but don't come back to my court no more."

More Boyhood Adventures

Chapter 37

We went back to school, but there warn't much excitement goin' on there, 'cept the teacher told us that the principal was comin' out there. She was a principal of the Leesburg Grammar School. She said, "Y'all better be on your best behavior. She's got a stick 'bout a foot long, and she'll beat the fire out of you if you ain't good." Well, I knowed I didn't want to be beat by no stick.

The principal come on Wednesday and come into the classroom. She talked to the teacher, but she didn't seem so bad. I didn't see no switch in her hand. She had a note book, but that was the only thang she had. Well, the week passed purty fast. But still nothin' excitin' happened.

Come Saturday mornin', I got my .22 and box of bullets. I told Byron, "Lets go down over there to the swamp. The water's run out quite a bit and maybe we can see that ole snake." So we went over, stopped by Uncle Will's, he said he was feelin' poorly.

"You been drinkin' too much of that wine."

He said, "I done drink all of that wine, boys. I'm tellin' you that's the best wine that I have ever drunk up in my life. You got to be careful. You drink too much and you pass out, though. You don't even know what's happenin'. I ain't never had no wine that good before."

We didn't tell 'im we put that shine in it. But I got a feelin' he knowed that anyway.

Then we left there and went down Stagecoach Road, crossed over the gate, went down to Cason Hammock, climbed up in the tree and layed down on our bed bunk. We layed there for a couple hours. Then Byron said, "Let's go walk that grove and see if we can see that snake."

We ain't seen nothin' since the fire. He was afraid that ole snake had burned up in the fire. But I warn't afraid, 'cause if it had to, that big ole snake would jist go under water. That's what most snakes do.

So we got out there and walked over to the gate and climbed back through the orange grove down past Lake Denham. We walked by the banana trees and walked on down where we ended up in the swamp.

I said, "Well, let's walk down there by the edge of the swamp." So we walked down through the logs and walked in there; it didn't look like anythin' was goin' on. But the skeeters was out, so we walked back on out and went down towards the spring.

We didn't see no snake tracks, and we said, "That ole snake is gone, probably burned up in that fire ole Bill set."

So we went up to the spring and shucked our clothes. We swam a little bit, saw a moccasin; got that with a .22 and killed it. He was a cotton mouth; they's nasty! They say that they won't bite you in water, but I don't trust it. Then we put our clothes back on; they's always a little wet, but they dry out purty quick. We walked up northwest; still didn't see no snake tracks. We come back through by the springs and still didn't see none.

Byron said, "We might as well go back and swim in the spring." So we got back in there, shucked our clothes again, kicked some sand around and washed ourselves off good and washed our feet.

Got out of the springs, put our clothes on, eased back through there and saw a possum. She had two little ones. They warn't on their tail like it shows in them books. They was hangin' from her hair. She could run fast too. She couldn't see us. We was still in redskin, but it was comin' off purty good. And she piddled along. Byron said, "You wanna catch the possum?"

I said, "No let her go." So they eased on down in the swamp and were gone unharmed. We went back through the orange grove. We still didn't see no snake tracks. We saw what looked like another dog been down in there though. And I thought, *Huh! We got more dog trouble again?*

Then we looked up and here come a fella; he was bird huntin'. And he had his bird dog with 'im. They was bird dog tracks we'd saw. He'd give 1 shot and the birds would go to the hammock. When they go to that hammock, then you can't find them. We told 'im, we said, "There's a bad snake down in that hammock." Said, "It'll kill that dog if that dog runs up to it."

He said, "Well, I'm fixin' to leave anyway. Ain't found no birds." We didn't tell 'im 'bout Cason Hammock 'cause we done trapped most of 'em and ate 'em. He went back up in his truck and went on down the road.

We went back to the hammock, climbed back up on it. Layed up there for three or four hours. All we saw come by was a few squirrels, 1 or 2 birds, and that was it.

We went back to Byron's house, went by the cow pen and I said, "I think I'm goin' home. It's gettin' late in the afternoon and I think I need to go home."

So I went home and they had supper fixin'. We et. I washed my face and thought I could get away with it, but it was Saturday. My mama said, "You ain't had your bath this week."

I said, "Uh-oh."

She said, "We done poured out the wash water, so you gonna have to pump you some wash water." So I went out there and got me a bucket and I pumped a bucketful. She said, "That ain't enough." So I pumped me another bucketful and I poured it in the tub. She asked me if I wanted to heat the water. And I said, "No, this is fine."

I been over there in that spring and that spring washin' would have been good enough. I went out there and took my bath and then poured out the rest of that water in the orange trees. I went to bed and slept like a log.

The next mornin' it was Sunday mornin', so we went to church. After church I told Byron, I said, "I'm goin' to go home and eat and then I'll come over."

We went down to the cow pen and swung on the swings. Then we come back to the house and Byron's youngest brother Jerry, he was 'bout 3 or 4 years old, had gotten to strikin' matches. An ole '36 Chevrolet car had been sittin' out in the field a long time. So he went out there and took the gas cap off. Then he took 1 of 'em matches and

throwed it in it, and the thang exploded. I mean it made a big noise!!!
It burned all the hair off Jerry's head and his eye lashes and it blew that
ole car up 'bout 5 foot off the ground and back down. We all thought
it was funny 'til Byron's mama come out there with a belt and whipped
Byron for lettin' 'im do it. It warn't Byron's fault. Maybe.

Well, I thought it was time for me to go home. Whenever all that
whippin's goin' on, it's time to go home. I don't want to be a part of it. I
went back over towards the field and went to my house. My mama and
daddy was sittin' on the porch and asked me, "What was that noise?"
And I said, "Aww, Byron's car blowed up."

He said, "Did you set it?"

"No, I didn't set it."

"Ok."

(Later in years, Jerry become Fire Chief of Leesburg.)

The Kaolin Mine

Chapter 38

The day was jist started. It was 'bout 6:00. My dad cooked break-fast, jist what I liked, fried eggs, them cat-eye biskits, fatback from the hog; I even got me some coffee. I mixed my eggs in grits and poured me some cane s'rup to sop with them cat-eye biskits. It don't get no better than this.

I told my dad I was was goin' to the creek by the railroad bridge to shoot some fish, if I could find some. He told me to bring 'em home.

I saw Byron comin' down the road. He had his .45-70 and 'bout 10 shells. I got my .22 and 'bout 20 shells. That should be enough. One would shoot and the other would jump in and grab any that come to the top. We took off down the railroad track. Them rocks was hard on our bare feet, but our feet was 'bout as tough as hog skin.

My mama fixed us four cat-eye biskits and put some of her guava jelly on 'em. She even gave Byron a sweet tater. She knowed he liked 'em.

We jist passed Worm Farm Road and was goin' east to the creek. It looked like it was gonna rain. The clouds was gettin' dark. So we saw the trussel where the train went over. The rain cloud was buildin' up purty dark, but if we could make it to the ole mine we could stay dry. So we hurried and went inside that big old building where it was dry.

When we stepped inside, we heared a rattlesnake shake his tail. We knowed he was there, but we couldn't see 'im. Then I seen 'is head; I raised my .22 and shot his head. That bullet ricocheted all around us, so we layed flat on the floor to keep it from hittin' us. You couldn't tell which way it went. Then Byron said that he heared another rattler. The 1 I shot was a Diamond Back. It'd jist shed its skin and was butter gold.

The storm got bad and the rain and wind blowed the trees every which way. But there was still another snake in there with us. Then we saw her; she was gold and butter-like, jist like the male. I told Byron we better kill her with a stick. "If I shoot, I don't know where the bullet will go. So we looked for a limb. Byron picked up a small limb and hit her on the head. She was a Heart Back."

We knowed not to pick up no snake. Byron held that snake head down and I took my pocket knife out and cut its head off. Even without its body it tried to bite us. We put the other head on a board and split the bottom of the snake. We pulled the hide off. "I bet the snake man will pay us $2.00 each for these. We looked to see if there was any more inside. The storm was goin' good, and there was nothin' that would burn outside, so we built us a good fire inside the mine.

This mine was where they dried the kaolin (clay for makin' pottery). It's a gray-lookin' clay; hard to dig with a shovel. They say they put it in tooth paste. I didn't know; I didn't have a tooth brush. My daddy told me to flatten a green stick and scrub my teeth that way. That's how they did it in World War I.

The kaolin mines closed before we was born. It was nice and warm in the mine. We washed our hands with dirt and rain water. Them snakes stink!! We got washed up, dried our hands on our pants. We sat down by the fire to have lunch. There was a tin can there so we caught us some rain water. We put it over the fire to boil so we wouldn't catch no worms; that would be bad for us.

I took that paper sack and gave Byron that sweet tater. He said, "Your mama sure do know what I like." I et 1 of them cat-eye biskits, drank some water and passed the can to Byron. He drank what was left.

The storm let up some, but it was still rainin'. We thought we'd jist sit it out. I give 'im 2 of 'em cat-eye biskits. We et it all. The rain stopped and we put the fire out. We sure didn't want to burn everythin' down.

"Let's go look at the creek," I said. It was muddy; no need to look for fish. The snakes that we had skinned was still movin'. They say they don't die 'til the sun goes down.

We left the mines and headed home 'bout 3:30. My daddy was workin' in the black smith shop. "Well, boys, how did you do?"

"We killed two big old rattlesnakes and skinned 'em," we said.

"Let me see 'em," he said.

We had 'em rolled up.

"Would you like for me to make you a belt each?"

We both said, "Yes." Byron had the Diamond Back and I had the Heart Back.

He cut the leather to fit us. He put that wet skin on Byron's belt and sewed it with cat gut fishin' line. He said, "They's no way to put the rattle on it." But he made a buckle from a round wire. It looked good but you had to let it dry. Then he made mine. We had the only rattlesnake belts in Oka-humpa, or maybe in the world!

My mama had fixed supper. "Let's eat," she said.

Byron said, "I gotta go home."

But I said, "She's got sweet taters."

"Let me wash my hands."

My mama made some apple turn-overs. My daddy killed a deer and Mama made a big pot of stew. I like that; they said grace and we et a belly full. I thought I had everythin'. The rich folk would probably like to have what I got.

Byron said he had better go 'cause it was gettin' late. But my mama wrote a note that said he had stayed late to eat supper. I walked 'im to the old post office and then I turned and went home. I washed my feet; my mama washed my arms and hands with that lard soap to get the snake smell off me. I was tired and went to bed. I layed in that feather bed and went sound asleep, but 'bout 11:30 my brother come home and he stuck his cold feet on me.

Then he said, "You stink! What have you been into now?" I jist smiled. Like I said, "Some day I'll get even with you."

The next mornin' I brought 'im a surprise. I handed 'im his draft notice.

(He went on to work on the trigger used on the A Bomb for the Manhattan Project.)

The Kaolin Mine

Cow Tales

Chapter 39

They was a man that lived on Bay Street in an old shack. He had two rooms in the house and an outdoor privy, jist like we had, and a pump in the back yard. He worked in the mines and made a dollar a day workin' in the mines way over in Sumterville. He walked there every day and then walked back every night.

If somebody picked 'im up, he'd take the ride, but usually there warn't nobody on that old state road. He'd come by the Red Hill Grove and 'cross that mud flat across there. He had to work; he had to eat. If you don't work, you don't eat. He had two little girls and they all lived on 5 dollars a week. I don't know what they paid in rent, probably a couple dollars a month, maybe five. Whatever it was, it was lots of money to 'im when he only made a dollar a day.

One day, instead of walkin' all the way around, he walked across that field where that man's white-faced cows was at. That man had 'im arrested for trespassin'! They took 'im to the Central and fined 'im 10 dollars. That's bout 2 weeks of work! That hurt! We heared 'bout it and we didn't think it was right. So Byron and I went there and cut them fences and drove them white-faced cows almost all the way to Sumterville. They was a fence across the road, so we couldn't have gotten them any farther. And we turned them loose and walked back home. I had climbed out the window. My brother wanted to know where I was at, but I said, "I can't tell you."

So the next day the sheriff showed up, and the man who owned the pasture was gonna put all the boys in Okahumpka in jail. A big ole German man said, "I want to tell you somethin' now. You arrest 1 of them boys, and I'll give everyone of 'em a box of .22 bullets, and you won't never have another cow in Okahumpka. They can shoot 'em at 200 yards and kill every one of 'em.

"Now, I'll tell you what you need to do. You can do it or not. You take and give that man back his 10 dollars, and you give 'im an old car of some kind, and all will be forgotten. But if you don't do that, you won't ever have another cow in Okahumpka. Every time you get 1, it'll die of gangrene. And you won't know how they do it. Now, I'll let you make up your mind what you want to do."

So he turned around and walked off.

The next day we saw 'im ridin' down the road in an old beat-up Chevrolet car, but it was runnin'. The farmer that had that was killed over on Hwy 27. He run the stop sign and someone hit 'im. But that's jistice. It was jistice for us.

The man at the dairy come by the house wanting to know if I'd like to go work at the dairy, wash bottles and clean up. I said, "Yeah."

He said, "I'll pay you ten cents an hour." I figured that was fair wages. So I went over there the next mornin' and went to work. He said, "Now this is 7 days a week. Every day them cows got to be milked."

I said, "Ok. I can do that." I go over there and he had 2 electric motors over there with brushes on them. You'd run the bottle up and soap it and wash it out. Then you'd put in over there and put the rinse wash on it. If you wanted to drink the milk you could have a cup free.

"They's a cup over there," he said. And it was good. But it never come with any of that ice that cools it.

We couldn't have none of that chocolate milk. That cost too much. Of course, we drank that too. We jist wouldn't let 'im know it. We'd get us 1 of them bottles and then drink it down. Then we'd wash the bottle and put it in the rack.

I did that for 'bout a month, and in the afternoons I had to clean up the cow manure on the floors, wipe down the walls, wipe down everythin'. Then I'd get 'bout 2 dollars. One mornin' I was runnin' 10 minutes late; I don't 'member why. I went over there and worked an hour and put my 2 hours in that afternoon. That shoulda been 30 cents, but he give me a nickel.

He said, "You was late to work today."

I said, "But I worked past time."

He said, "That don't make no difference. I don't put up with people bein' late to work." So he cheated me out of my afternoon job that I'd done and the mornin'. So I come home and tell my dad. I told 'im 'bout 'im cheatin' me out of 25 cents.

My dad said, "Well, don't go there and work for 'im anymore."

I saw Byron leavin' the store. I got 'im and we went down to the depot and we sat on the steps. I said, "What should I do? Should I go back to work and make that 30 cents a day? Or should I take and get even?"

He said, "Get even."

So I said, "What do you think I ought to do?"

He said, "I don't know."

I said, "What if I soak them bottles up and jist not rinse 'em?"

He said, "That'd be good. Nobody likes soapy milk."

I said, "That's what I'll do."

I went down the next mornin', on time, and I soaked them bottles up. I put 'em in the rack and worked that mornin' and that afternoon. He give me the 30 cents. I was thankful I got my money every day. That afternoon I looked up and he was sittin' at the house. He said, "This boy soaped them bottles up, but he didn't rinse 'em and it ruined all that milk. I got to make 'em all good."

My dad said, "Well, you shouldn't have cheated 'im out of his money."

He said, "Well, he was late that day."

Dad said, "You don't have to worry 'bout it any more. He won't be there."

He said, "I know he won't. You gonna pay for that milk."

Dad said, "I ain't payin' for nothin."

He said, "Oh, well, somethin' gonna happen."

"Sure is."

He said, "I might jist whip you."

"I might jist shoot you."

He got in his ole Model A and drove off down the road.

My dad said, "Boy, don't go there anymore."

I told 'im, "Yes, sir."

I always wondered what them people thought when they drank that milk that was soapy.

The Red Dog

Chapter 40

Byron and I went down to the store and we was sittin' down on the bench out in front of the store. My daddy had got me a dog, a big ole red hound. He had floppy ears and was good natured as he could be. But anytime any one would get around you he'd show his teeth. He wouldn't bite nobody, but everybody thought he would. I liked that. So we was sittin' there and the ole dog was sittin' next to us. He liked cold drinks too. You could pour it out and he'd drink it right up. We found some gin 1 day that we was goin' to give to Uncle Will. Somebody hid it in that burnt-out oak tree in the middle of the road.

We was jist sittin' there and got to talkin'. Byron said, "I wonder, can that dog get drunk?" I said, "If you get a bottle and turn it up, he'll drink it 'cause he'll think its 1 of them soda waters. We'll grab his mouth and hold 'im and he'll have to either drink it down or drown."

Byron said, "Sounds like a winner."

We took that-there gin and we walked over there to give 'im a little drink out of the bottle. Then we got the other 1 and he was all for it. I stuck it up there on his tongue. He sort of leaned sideways and when he did I grabbed a hold of 'im and held 'im. He could either drink or drown. He decided to drink. He drunk 'bout half of that bottle. I thought it was funny. We put the gin back in the tree over there with the lid on it. We started home and I noticed the dog warn't walkin" straight. His back legs didn't quite measure up with his front legs.

Byron said he was goin' home. So I come on home with the red dog. We walked down Main Avenue and went across the railroad track. That ole house we have is 'bout 2 foot off the ground. I looked underneath the house after the dog went under it. He didn't look like he felt too good. He layed in there and I went in to supper and on to bed. "Bout 9 o'clock that ole dog needed to howl. He turned loose, "Aoooo. Aoooo."

My dad come in and said, "Go out there and get that dog. I don't know what's wrong with 'im."

So I went out there and carried 'im out. He couldn't walk. I took 'im to the barn and put 'im in the hay. I didn't have to worry 'bout 'im. There warn't nothin' out there 'cept snakes and rats, that kind of stuff. The next mornin' I went out to the barn and there he was. His eyes were 'bout as bloodshot as they could be. He looked like he'd been on 2 drunks instead of 1.

We went to the store 'bout a week later and I got me a pink soda water. Me and Byron split it 'cause we only had 1 nickel. I used up all the money I made at the dairy.

He said, "Where's the dog?"

I said, "He's sittin' right here."

"He want a sip of this?"

I said, "Yeah, give 'im a sip."

He said, "Come here. Good gracious, look at his eyes."

I said, "Yeah, they bloodshot. He was all drunk."

"Here, want some of this?"

That ole dog run around and hid behind the bench.

"He don't want no more of that!! He done all the drinkin' he wants."

Never Forget "The Snake"

Chapter 41

We run over behind Byron's house 'cause we was gonna possum hunt. The possum would climb up a tree, and we'd take a bamboo pole and poke up there to get 'im out. Then we'd put 'im in a sack. But we couldn't figure out what to do with 'im.

Everybody said, "Oh you can sell 'im." Ain't nobody gonna buy a possum. But Jack Whitaker did. Jack caught possums and sold them. He had a pen down there, so every night we'd go get possums, and we'd put 'em in his pen. He'd sell 'em for a nickel apiece. He'd fatten them up and sell 'em.

We was still thinkin' 'bout that snake, so one night we said, "Let's spend the night in the hammock." So we got our pillows; Byron got his .45-70 and I got my .22 and we headed down and went by Uncle Will's. He told us not to go down there at night, but it was a moonlit night and we could see everythin'. We climbed up in the tree and got on our bunks. It would've been really nice to have a blanket over us, but when you're that young, it don't matter.

We layed up there and watched the night pass by. We seen ole coons with two little ones; a dog come by, but it belonged to someone. We don't need to shoot that one; it won't harm nothin'. Then we heard this noise and thought, "Oh boy, here comes our snake." We was finally gonna get 'im! You could hear 'im comin', and he'd make a little noise and then stop. He'd rub up against the grass and stop. And then it come out. It was that ole HOG!

He had all them holes on his ears; I guess he never learned. He was foamin' at his mouth. He smelled us. He knowed we was there somewhere, but he didn't know where. He stunk so bad, you could smell 'im, and we knowed that we didn't want to kill 'im. He warn't hurtin' us. We layed there 'til 'bout midnight and then went to sleep. We woke up the next mornin' and climbed down. We'd brought 2 eggs over there, and we put a little bit of lard in the fryin' pan. We cooked 'em hard where we could jist reach in and eat 'em. We said, "Next time we'll bring us some flour and we'll make us some biskits."

We walked through the groves lookin' for snake tracks. We walked in and got into Lake Denham Swamp. We got across the logs and climbed up in the stand and layed down up there. That warn't as easy here as it was at the other place. We'd lay on the hard floor, and we had a gun rest, where we could shoot whatever. Out come Ole Joe, the alligator. He swum by. We watched 'im swim up the canal. We layed there for 4 to 5 hours, but nothin' more come by. Then we heared a noise. Now it was 'bout 4 o'clock in the afternoon. I said, "You know what, if that snake comes by now, we won't hardly have time to skin 'im. But if he comes by we'll still kill 'im."

We got all primed and ready, and Byron said, "Now if I shoot and miss..."

"You ain't gonna miss."

"You kill 'im with that .22"

I said "Ok." But out walked that ole sow with 'bout 10 little bitty pigs, I mean little bitty ones. He said, "Oh, look at that!"

Well, Ole Joe spied 'em too. I said, "Don't let Ole Joe get 'em."

So Byron fired that rifle "POW!" The bullet landed jist 'bout a foot from Ole Joe's head. He jumped right out of the water and went back across there. Then we went on up, looked around and still didn't see nothin' else.

So we climbed right out of the stands, waded back across the logs and come into the orange grove. Guess what? There was the snake tracks. He had went toward Cason Hammock. Now, it was almost 5 o'clock and we knowed it would be dark in a little bit. We didn't want to get caught in that swamp in the dark down on the ground. So we went on by Uncle Will's. He warn't there. We don't know where he was at. So we come back by Byron's house. He went in the house and I went over across the field to my house. I washed my face and my hands and my feet. I et supper and went to bed.

The week went by purty quick. It was Saturday again and we walked off down to the store to get us some Black Cow candy bars. We scraped up a nickel and got a big one. A penny would only get us a little one. So we got the big one. We was sittin' out front on the bench there and this black lady walked up and said, "I heared you boys is chasin' that snake."

We said, "We sure are."

She said, "I saw it the other day and it scared the mud out of me."

We said, "Where did you see it?"

She said, "You know where the island's at in Lake Denham?"

We said, "Yeah, we know where the island's at."

"Right out there on the island. We was fishin' around and we looked up and it raised it head up. It went down towards the Lake Denham Swamp."

We said, "When was that?"

She said, "Friday afternoon."

We said, "Huh! We were there Saturday mornin' but didn't see no tracks."

She said, 'It's a big snake. It's a big ole rattle."

We said, "Oh, did y'all come from the landin' down there?"

She said, "Where somethin' landed."

We said, "Yeah, we know where it's at."

She said, "What kind of stuff you got over there in them woods? I hear a drum beatin'. I hear the weirdest sounds comin' from over there."

"I don't know," we said. "We'll look into that island thang. We're lookin' for 'im. We're gonna kill 'im as soon as we find 'im."

She said, "I hope you do. That thang's big. My sister and me ain't never seen a snake that big."

Byron said, "Let's go see what's over there." So I went by my house and got my .22 and he got his .45-70, and we both grabbed a handful of bullets. We didn't load our guns in the boat; that was too dangerous. We'd take our poles sometime and catch some fish. Byron'd catch all the bass. So we was purty well loaded down. We went by Uncle Will's before we went down over there and we told 'im what we were goin' to do. He said that if we caught 'im some nice fish he'd cook 'em for us.

So we went over there and got our boat. We turned left and went toward Lake Denham but didn't see nothin', 'cept a few gators and a couple of otters. We'd like to have 'em. We'd make an otter-skin cap. You can take that thang and form it around a stump. You put the tail in the back and you make it any size you want according to what size stump you put it over. But, we didn't shoot 'em; we let 'em go.

We went back on down towards the swamp where we got to our stand and back up by Sutton's Landing in Lake Denham. Then we come along the island and you could see where that snake was on that island. We got to lookin' to find out what way it'd gone. North, from the track we seen. We looked all around and there was another track there. It looked like it'd gone north too. That means that snake's crossin' here. Maybe we ain't doin' this thang wrong after all. Maybe we ought to get out here and sit on the island.

Next Saturday, we got our rifles and we'd come out here and fish for blue gill fish where they always was. We paddled all around the lake and said, "Well, let's go up the run a little ways and see if there's anythin' up there."

We went up the run a little ways and a few wood ducks jumped up. I said, "If we ease around that bend, there's a wood duck down there. I'll kill it and we'll take and barbecue it."

Byron said, "Ok."

We eased around the bend and I told 'im, "Stop!" and I shot that thang.

He said, "What'd you kill?"

I said, "I don't know."

He said, "You know how to skin it?"

I said, "No, I ain't never killed one of 'em before." We went up there and he said "That's a goose!"

I said, "A goose?"

He said, "Yeah, a goose."

So I said, "Well, are we gonna cook it or what are we gonna do?"

He said, "I'd take that thang home and let your mama bake it."

I said, "That ain't a bad idea." Said, "We'll save them feathers and we'll take Larry's buzzard feathers out and we'll put 'em in our headdress. If my mama knowed I'd put buzzard feathers in my headdress, she'd beat the fire out of me."

Then we left and paddled back over by the island again. Didn't see nothin'. I was pickin' the feathers off and puttin' 'em in the water. You could see in the water. Every once in a while an ole mudfish would come along. He'd see a feather and he'd grab it and spit it out. We paddled down Bugg Spring Run, pulled them boats up in that cove there.

We got out, walked through the woods and he said, "Well, you need to take that goose home with you."

So I took the goose home and told my mama I'd killed this goose over there and wondered if she could cook it.

She said, "I never cooked goose before, but I cooked lots of duck. It probably wouldn't be any different." So I took the guts out of it and the heart and the liver, cleaned the gizzard, and then I throwed the guts and stuff in the hog pen. The hogs et it all. I went back in the house and gave the goose to my mama and she put it in the pan to let the grease run out of it.

I said, "I don't know why the grease is in it." I found out that goose had more grease in it than you could shake a stick at. So then she baked it up and made some dressin'. Saturday night we had goose and dressin'. Byron come over and et too. I didn't particularly like it, but it's better than nothin'. We had that and water and then Byron went on home.

I had to take a bath 'cause it was Saturday. I didn't want to do that either, but it was 1 of them thangs I had to do. I was still concerned 'bout that ole snake. I took my bath and went to bed. I was tired and didn't dream nothin'.

How to Catch Bluegills

Chapter 42

The week went by with not much excitement at all. We decided we'd go back over to the islands to dig us some earth worms and get us a pole and we'd fish while we waited for the snake to come. So I got up 'bout 5 o'clock that mornin' and went to Byron's. I had my .22 and a can of worms we'd dug up underneath that ole oak tree. I had my straw hat, my long sleeved shirt and my gloves, so I wouldn't get sunburned.

Byron paddled the boat down out of Bugg Spring and we went into Lake Denham. We crossed the land and there was a light fog, but you could see purty well. We eased around a corner and found a fish bed right off the bat. A whole bed as big as a bucket! If you drop that bait in that hole, you'd catch a bluegill. We waited around there and kept watchin' the lake hopin' to see the snake. But we didn't see no snake. We stayed there 'til 'bout 10 o'clock. We was catchin' bluegills and even turnin' 'em loose when this-here boat come by. She asked us, "You catchin' any fish?"

We said, "Yes."

She said, "Cause we ain't." They showed us the line they was usin'. It was big ole wire with a hook on the end. Her husband was sittin' in the back of the boat.

Byron said, "You jist ain't hooked up right." Said, "Let me show you how to do it."

So he put on a smaller hook and shortened her cork up; put 1 of them earthworms on and dropped the line right in that blue gill bed. It went "thunk" and went under. But before he put the hook on he spit on the hook. She said, "Why are you spittin' on the worm?"

Byron said, "'Cause that's what makes the fish bite."

"Oh, Ok." That thang didn't even slow down. She got a big ole blue gill and brought it between me and Byron. She put it over there and he put another worm on, spit on the hook, dropped it in that hole and "thunk". It went right down. She done that 'bout10 or 12 times and Byron said, "Well, we need to go. You want these earthworms?"

"Yeah!" she said. "Do you spit on that worm every time?"

"Every time. If'n you don't spit on that worm you don't get no fish. As long as you spit on that thang, you'll catch them fish."

We went back out real easy so that we didn't disturb that fish bed. Her husband was sittin' in the back of the boat and he said, 'You ain't believin' them, are you?"

She said, "Yep. How many fish you caught?"

He said he hadn't caught none. She'd caught ten and was catchin 'em comin' and goin'. What she didn't realize was that she was fishin' in the bed, and he was fishin' there out in the open.

We paddled back across Lake Denham and went back across the run. We come back down by the landin' there and went by Helena Run. We got up on the bank and cleaned the fish; cut the heads off. We got all the mud off 'em and rubbed 'em off good. We put 'em in that little feed sack we had and went over to Uncle Will's.

Uncle Will said, "Boys, you must-a catched a bunch of 'em thangs." We said, "Oh yeah, there's a bed over there. We catched 'em in that bed."

So he said, "Well, how many you think you gonna eat?"

We said, "Why don't you cook us up 1 each."

He said, "I'll do that."

He poured the lard in his pan and salt and pepper and fired it up. Whenever it was done we layed it out on an old piece of tin he had right out there on the table and we let it cool a little bit. We ate our fish. I told Byron, I said, "We better be goin' home."

He said, "Yeah, it's gettin' late." Still we hadn't seen that snake. But we knowed it's there. We knowed it didn't burn up in that fire. That fire burned purty good through there. You could go right through where we come. It burned all through there. You could look out and see all the snakes. He said, "I'll tell you what, one day we go out there and we'll shoot all the snakes."

I said, "Fine with me." We don't shoot anythin' we don't kill or skin. But moccasins is bad news and we'll get them down a little bit by shootin' 'em. You won't kill 'em all, but you'll slow them down a little bit.

So I left Byron's house and walked across the field. I carried 3 of them fish home with me and Byron carried 3 with 'im; Uncle Will had 2 of 'em and we each et one. When I got home my dad said, "Well, we'll fry 'em up for supper."

I said, "Don't fry 1 for me; I already et supper." So he fried 'im 1 and 1 for my mama and they made some grits and used the grease off the fish fryin' to put in the grits. She had some cold biskits there and she warmed 'em on top of the ole woodstove to warm 'em real quick. They kinda dry up when you do that though. Then she gives 'em a shot of butter inside and a shot of jam. They ain't bad.

So I washed my face and I washed my hands and I washed my feet and I went to bed.

Saved by Ole Joe

Chapter 43

The next mornin' I got up and thought, *Well, I'll go over by Byron's and we'll go in the swamp.* We hadn't been in there too much recently. We gonna have to find where that snake was and kill it, 'cause if we don't, somebody else is gonna kill it and we gonna lose that hundred dollars. So we got up and went into the swamp. Byron said, "Where do you wanna go?"

I said, "I wanna go to Lake Denham Swamp down there."

And he said, "I believe we go down there more than anywhere else."

We went down the road by Uncle Will's; he hadn't got up yet. So we went on down by the canal and went on down Stagecoach Road and climbed over the gate. He said, "Nah, don't go over there. That's Cason Hammock. Let's go down there to the swamp like we started."

So we went on down to the swamp and walked in on the log. We looked up, and there was Bill in that thang we built up high in the tree! He was layin' up in there. We eased back and Byron said, "I ought to shoot 'im."

But I said, "No, don't do that. They'll put us in jail."

He said, "Well, I still wanna shoot 'im."

We went to school all next week but warn't nothin' excitin' happenin'. We jist went there. They didn't mention the War of 1812, so I guess that war had been taught enough. We knowed Saturday was comin' up, so he said, "What are we goin' to do Saturday?"

Said, "I don't know, but we'll do somethin'."

He said, "Do you want to take the float and go by Lake Denham?"

I said, "Yeah, we can do that. We can go into the hammock and see what's in there."

He said, "Aw, let's go floatin'."

I said, "That's fine with me."

So Saturday mornin' I arrived over at his house 'bout 9 o'clock with my .22, and he took his .45-70. We hid 'em in the woods; we didn't want to take 'em on the float 'cause we figured we'd lose 'em. And if we lost 'em we could never replace 'em.

We went down Bugg Spring Run, went to Helena Run and took a left. Up there, we eased along the edge and said, "Let's go by the island."

So we started out there and went by the island, and lo and behold, Ole Joe stuck out in the grass and grabbed the front of our float! Byron was over on that side and he beat 'im upside the head with that push pole. Ole Joe was a chewin' and grindin' and we said, "What's he tryin' to do, kill us?" And then it happened!

That big ole snake crawled right out in front of us headed for Cason Hammock. I mean he was gettin' there fast. We finally got Joe away from the front of the boat, but we was shakin'. We didn't know what to do, so we headed back down Helena Run. Our float was sinkin' on 1 side real bad, so we got down Helena Run and thought if we could get down the side real easy, then we could go to Spring's Run, walk through the sawgrass in there right back to where our guns is at; and then we'd go kill that snake.

We got back up to where we pulled the boat in and put it on the bank. It was sinkin' so bad on that 1 side that it wouldn't hold up. We tried to pull it up but we couldn't. It was too full of water. It wouldn't go nowhere. If we turned it loose, it would jist go to the bottom. Said, "We'll jist get it out later."

We grabbed our guns and run up to where we had our little house up in the trees in Cason Hammock. We climbed up. Not a sound. Nothin'. We layed there for 'bout an hour and a half. Nothin' happened.

We said, "You know that Ole Joe, was he tryin' to save us from that snake? Or was he jist mad at us 'cause we been tryin' to get that snake and he wanted to get that snake? I don't know which one it was but I'll tell you 1 thang, he sure did mess up our float."

Byron said, "You know what? I think he was tryin' to save us. He might have been. We jist went right on in where that snake was at. Let's go in the grove and see if that snake is in there."

We went in the grove but didn't see no snake tracks. We went all the way up past Knights Landing and sat on the landin'. We went straight on up almost to the end and still no track. So we decided we'd go right on up to the end of Lake Denham Swamp. We went up where the old log lay in the water, and we walked across the log and walked in the swamp. We looked up there, and we could see where Byron shot that limb off. We climbed up there on it; it was quiet. The swamp's not usually that quiet. Said, "That snake's here somewhere. It's here. It's close by. And if it don't move a bush, we won't never see it."

Byron got his rifle all ready and said, "If it's runnin', I can kill it runnin'."

I tell 'im, "Ok." He'd probably shoot the head off it. That's fine. We layed there probably for an hour, then the bushes was shakin'.

Said, "Here he comes."

We watched and could see the bushes movin', movin', movin', and he was comin' towards us. He was gettin' closer and closer, but out walked that ole boar hog!! He musta smelled us in the woods and here he come. He was a foamin' at the mouth, which they do if they smell somebody and don't know where they's at.

I thought, *You know what, one day we gonna have to shoot 'im; he aggravates us more than anythin' else in this swamp, but he don't bother us. I guess we ought not bother 'im.*

"That Ole Joe really tore that float up. I think it probably sunk to the bottom by now."

He said, "I don't think it probably sunk to the bottom. We'll go there and pull it out and see if we can fix it."

He chewed the whole front end off it and got most of the bamboo. I was scared when he did that.

So we stayed up there 'bout another hour and a half. Nothin' come by and that ole boar went on off through the woods. I guess he was headin' south. A couple of coons come by and was lookin' for food. It was lookin' a little bit like rain so, we said, "Let's go to Uncle Will's." So we went to Uncle Will's and told 'im what happened 'bout the gator bitin' the front of the float.

"That big ole snake was up there on that little island," he said. "You boys need to stay away from that place."

We told 'im, "Well, we can't go out on the float no more; he tore that thang up. And I don't think we can fix it. I guess it's a good thang, 'cause eventually one of us would have fell off and drowned."

He said, "Well, y'all see the snake?"

We said, "Yeah, it was 'bout 20 feet from us. It crawled over there toward Cason Hammock, but when we went there we didn't see 'im there. We didn't see nothin'. Then we got down and went to the other stand and climbed up in it; the only thang we come by there was that ole boar hog."

Said, "You think maybe they know you up in them stands?"

Said, "We know they know we're up there. They know and that ole boar hog was foamin' at the mouth. That was tellin' us he either smelt us or saw us. And we seen Ole Joe, the gator."

Byron said we should have shot that thang a long time ago. Maybe he was right, maybe he was wrong. That gator might've been protectin' us from the big ole snake.

It was late and we needed to get home.

Uncle Will said he sure would like some of that swamp water. We told 'im we'd see what we could do. We hadn't been over there much since old Bill come and burned it up. We went on by the hog pen, crossed by the cow pen and walked behind Byron's house.

I said, "I'll see tomorrow at church."

I left 'im there and went home. Bath time again! I didn't say nothin' 'cause I knowed if'n I didn't say nothin', I wouldn't get in trouble. I went ahead and took my bath and went in. They fried up some bass that dad caught and had some grease gravy and some grits. I put 2 or 3 of them ole biskits on the stove so they'd warm up. Then I put some jelly in 'em so they tasted better. I et my supper and layed down in bed; slept like a dream.

Got up Sunday mornin' and went down to church and Sunday School. Then my mama informed me I should come home for Sunday dinner. I got home and she fried up some chicken. We had some green beans. They'd got some ice Saturday, so we had iced tea.We still had some cat-eyed biskits left over from breakfast. She layed 'em on the stove to warm up. They's good. Sometimes she'd put jelly in 'em; sometimes nothin'. I liked 'em any way. Sometimes she put butter in 'em before she put 'em on the stove and some brown sugar in them. They's always good.

We et lunch and my dad layed out on the porch to take a nap, which he did every Sunday afternoon. Then the man who did the dairy and the man who delivered the mail come by. They played checkers all afternoon. They never did win. Nobody ever did win a game but they played all afternoon. Sometimes we'd go over and watch 'em.

But I jist layed around the house that day, then went over to the hog pen and scratched the side of that ole hog. I listened to her grunt and groan back there. They's 'bout 25-30 pounds now; they's growin' fast.

I went back in the house, put my Sunday clothes back on and went to church that night.

The Big Shot

Chapter 44

Before I got ready to go, I was sittin' out on the porch. A man drove by. It was the man that Byron shot for down there and shot the turkey. He said, "Boy, where's your gun-shootin' partner?"

I said, "I'm gonna see 'im in a little bit; he gonna be at church."

He said, "There's a shoot-off this Saturday, up in Okella. I'll come and get y'all and take you up there."

I said, "Well, he's 'bout shot off all his bullets."

He said, "That's Ok. I'll get you some; don't worry 'bout that. You think he can go?"

I said, "Oh, I'm sure he can. But he needs to ask his mama first." I said, "Where in Okella are we goin'?"

He said, "To the National Forest. They got a gun range up there and they gonna have the best of the best. I figured your friend can beat the best of the best."

I said, "Ok. I'll tell 'im when I see 'im tonight. I'm sure he can go."

He said, "I'll pick y'all up at your house 'bout 7 o'clock."

I said, "That'll be fine. I need to make me a lunch."

He said, "Oh, no. I'll buy lunch. We'll go up there and we'll have a good time. Tell 'im to bring his .45-70 and bring his shootin' eyes."

I said, "We can do that."

So Sunday night I told Byron. I said, "Byron, next Saturday they havin' a shootin' up in Okella. That man wants you to come up there with your .45-70 and do some shootin'."

He said, "I can do that."

I said, "Ok. Be at my house at 7 Saturday mornin'."

He said, "Should I wear my good clothes?"

I said, "I don't know. I guess I'll go barefooted like I always do, like I am right now."

He said, 'Ok, jist wear my regular old huntin' clothes then."

I said, "Yeah."

The week went by purty fast. There warn't nothin' excitin' happenin'. But Saturday mornin' Byron was there 'bout 6:45. A few minutes later that man drove by. He had a fine automobile. He said, "You boys can ride up front if you want to."

We said, "You don't mind us gettin' in with no shoes on?"

He said, "No. You got your rifle? Well, I got you a couple of boxes of shells. I wanted you to shoot with new shells. What I want you to do is, the first shot I want you to miss."

I said, "Why do you want 'im to miss?"

That man said, "Well, there's gonna to be a lot of money on this thang. If you miss the first shot, then they'll think they have a good shot at winnin'."

Byron says, "I ain't never missed."

"Well, they'll be somethin' you can shoot at and see if you can get it."

"That'll be fine."

I said, "You got to watch it purty close up here. I'll check the nails to see if they be crooked and rusted."

Said, "Ok."

So we went up to the Okella National Forest and there was a hundred people up there. They was all kinds of fancy rifles and fancy clothes. We got out of the car and they looked like they was thinkin', "Where did these hicks come from?"

It cost a dollar a shot. We was gonna shoot for a Henry rifle. That man took us up there and he said, "Now boys, I want that Henry rifle. I'll tell you what, you get me that Henry rifle and I'll give both of you a .22 pistol."

Said, "Hmm. Never had a .22 pistol."

Well, we went down in there and they was some good shots. I mean they was shootin' targets!

Byron said, "Ok."

That man said, "Shoot the Number 1 on the target way up there at the top."

He said, "Ok."

He layed down there and "POW!" right dead center of the Number 1. That man had bet 20 dollars Byron could hit that bull's eye.

The guy come up and said, "Well, do you want to shoot again?"

He said, "Yeah!"

The guy said, "We might as well make this worthwhile. I'll put a hundred dollars he hits the bull's eye."

That man said, "How many of them hundred dollars will you cover?"

The guy said, "How many do you got?"

That man said, "Tell you what. I'll bet you 500 dollars he don't hit no bulls eye." 500 dollars!!!

Byron said, "Tell 'im, Yup."

That man said, "Boy, you think he can hit that bull's eye?"

I said, "Yes, he can."

That man said, "Ok. The closest one to the dot in the center wins."

The guy come out with that fancy lookin' rifle, with a big ole swoop on the center. His hand was on the back and he had a special lookin' thang on his shoulder where he shot from. They layed down in the position and lay it up on that log. Then he fired. It hit the bulls eye, but it was all the way over in the corner of it.

Byron took that ole .45-70 and that man handed 'im a bullet from the new box of bullet. Byron went "POW!"

Dead center!!! He says, "Huh! Dead center!"

"Dead center!"

The guy says, "Aw it was a lucky shot, warn't it?" He said, "You gonna let me win my money back? Are you?"

That man said, "Yeah, let's make it back. How 'bout drivin' a nail?"

Byron said, "Tell 'im, Ok."

Byron walked up there and looked. I said, "We need to make sure it's the right nail, 'cause he'll shoot the right nail."

The guy said, "Oh no, no. We gonna shoot the right nail."

Byron said, "You're tryin' to cheat me. It's in a knot on the left side."

And we all walked up there and looked. We said, "Yup, sure is."

Said to the guy, "You the 1 to put the nails in? You take the left side and I'll take the right." That fella layed down there and "BAM" he hit it on the left but he drove it. He drove it probably in 'bout 3 or 4 inches.

Byron layed down there with his little .45-70. "POW!" That nail went slam up to the hilt!

The guy said, "You broke it off." So they took a hatchet and chopped down; sure enough the nail was there."

The guy said, "How long you been shootin', boy?"

Byron said, "I didn't have to be taught. It warn't no trouble to learn. All you do is aim it down there and pull the trigger."

He said, "How much you take for your rifle?"

He said, "Ain't for sale."

He said, "I'll swap you a new rifle for it."

Byron said, "I don't want a new one. This one shoots too good."

So then they was gonna have a shoot-off for a new pair of boots.

The man said, "I'll pay the boy and you can have the boots."

So we got up there and sure enough they drove them nails in. I walked up there and looked at 'em. They all seemed purty evened out. I painted the ends white. Four of them shot and never touched 1 of them.

Then the shoot was offerin' the boots. He said, "Boy, can you drive two of them? I'll give you two pairs of boots."

I thought, *Hmm, I'll get a pair of 'em too.*

Byron said, "I think so." So he put five bullets in his rifle. Layed down there and "Pow! Pow! Pow! Pow! Pow!" He drove all five of 'em up to the hilt!

Now you've seen a bunch of wide-eyed ole men with a bunch of fancy rifles standin' around watchin' a nine-year ole boy drive nails in a log.

He said, "Where'd you learn to shoot like that?"

"Down in the swamp in Okahumpka."

He said, "Well, hmm."

He said, "He wants a pair of boots, too."

They said, "Ok, we'll give 'im a pair of boots too."

They was fancy boots. They had a knife in the boot, an itty-bitty knife. And then they had a whet rock in the thang with a button on top.

They was lace-up boots. And he gave us both a pair of boots and then he give Byron a jacket. "Best shot in the Okella National Forest."

They shot 4-5 different rounds in there and then he said, "Boys, want to do a little bettin'?"

"What kind of bettin' you want to do?"

"Oh, well, we'll drive nails, shoot targets, whatever." Said, "I'll shoot a hundred yards."

Byron said, "Tell 'im, "Ok."

Byron said, "Do I get a practice shot?"

He said, "Oh yeah, you get a practice shot." Said,"How much do you want to shoot for, boy?"

A guy said, "Oh, 50 dollars a shot, 5 shots. Who can do it the quickest and the best."

Byron said, "But you got an automatic rifle."

He said, "I'll give you 2 minutes."

Said, "You got it."

The man layed down there and, Bam, Bam, Bam, Bam, Bam.

We went down there and got the target but he didn't hit what he thought he did.

So Byron layed down and Bam, Bam, Bam, Bam, Bam. He went and got all five targets. Byron hit the center every time. The other fella, he'd been off to the right a little bit and then a bit to the left.

"Listen, boy, you good! I wonder what you could do with a good rifle."

Byron said, "I got a good rifle." Said, "This thang shoots where I put it. I don't miss very often. Sometimes I do 'cause everybody misses every once in a while."

They said, "Well, we gonna shoot off for the Henry rifle." Said, "I guess you gonna shoot, boy."

"Yeah, we gonna shoot for it."

So that man went up and paid for Byron's three shots.

He shot three times in dead center and hit it every time. They had a fella there with a rifle, called it a Browning. The rifle had a big stock on it. A fellow layed out his tripod and set down his rifle and fired. He hit it three times, dead center.

Now we was in a shoot-off. So they put up 5 targets and he shot 5 times. He hit 2 of 'em a little bit off. But Byron shot dead center 5 times!! Whew Doggie!

That fella said, "You the best there is, boy." Said, "I'll tell you what. I'd like to take you when we do a little tourin' shootin.'"

Byron said, "I can't do it right now. I have to go to school and my mama makes me go to school."

He said, "That's fine."

They presented the Henry rifle to Byron, but he said, "I had an agreement with that man, that if I won it, he could have it."

He said, "You did?"

Byron said, "Yes, I did. And I'm gonna keep my word, 'cause that's what we do in Okahumpka."

That fella said, "Ok. We got a fella here from Remington Arms that's gonna do a demonstration. He's got an automatic .22 and he's gonna make an Injun Head." Said, "He'd like for you to shoot his rifle and see if you can make that Injun Head."

Byron said, "Well, I don't know if I can or not. I don't know what an Injun Head looks like."

Said, "We'll draw it out with chalk. Then you draw it out with the .22." Byron raised that .22 and put it out on that piece of aluminum, "bam, bam, bam, bam, bam, bam, bam, bam, bam and it run out of shells. He filled it up and shot the rest of it. It warn't as good as the Remington Arms man, but it warn't bad.

The man said, "With a little trainin', boy, you can be the best there's ever been."

Byron said, "But you know what? I don't like to shoot that. I can take my .45-70 and I can make that Injun Head."

The guy said, "This thang shoots so good."

A fellow said, "Well, I know that. It's all 'bout what you get used to. If it warn't, I'd work for the Remington Rifle. I'd buy yours from you."

"Well, it ain't for sale." He said, "I'm gonna kill that big ole snake with this thang. We got a big ole thirty-foot rattle snake that we've been chasin' for almost a year. Eventually, we gonna kill 'im. And we gonna sell 'im to the snake man in Okella up there for a hundred dollars. He already says he'd pay us for it. We almost got 'im bout 2 or 3 times, but every time we almost got 'im, he gets away from us."

So they all gathered around and they had some barbecue there. We et us some barbeque. It was good.

That man said, "Go ahead, but don't eat too much though, cause we gonna stop at the steakhouse. You boys done good today."

We got up to the steakhouse. I ain't never ordered nothin' at a restaurant. I've never et in no restaurant. I didn't know how to order.

They said, "Well, you want steak?"

I said, "I reckon."

So Byron, he said he wanted a steak and he wanted it done. I did the same. I never had to eat one any other way. We always cooked 'em hard as a rock. So he orders the steak and I don't know what he told 'em but we got us a salad, a Coca Cola. Whew! That steak was good. I chomped down on that thang. The 2 eggs I et for breakfast with grits had done wore off. We drank 2 of them Cokes and I thought I would explode.

He rode us down to Silver Springs and we got out at Silver Springs. He bought us a ticket and we went out on the glass-bottom boat. He said, "I got somethin' I want to show you boys."

I'd never been there before. When I seen them catfish, I said, "Oooh, Byron, if we would get them thangs, we could cook 'em up."

That man said, "They won't let you fish in here."

Said, "Oh well, we'll fish here at nighttime."

That man said, "I got somebody I want you to meet. This is the snake man of Okella."

We looked at 'im and he said, "Where 'bouts you boys live?"

We said, "We live in Okahumpka. We been chasin' that big snake."

He said, "I heared 'bout it. And there's been a bunch of people chasin' it."

We said, "That thang's smart. We been within 20 feet of it with no rifle. We tryin' to kill 'im. He already killed my dog. He slipped them fangs up through the top of his head and they come out the bottom." Said, "He's a bad snake." And Ole Joe Gator saved us from 'im once. Chewed up our float." Said, "We gonna catch that snake. We gonna kill 'im and we gonna skin 'im and then we gonna call you."

He said, "I'd buy the hide. I'd buy that hide."

He said, "Hey, boys, wait now. You ever seen anyone milk a rattle-snake?"

We said, "No."

He run over there and grabbed a stick he had with a little bend in it behind the head. He put it on but not much come out of the snake. That surprised me. He said, "It makes the snake awful weak. If you milk 'im too much he'll die. You know when the rattlesnake kills, it uses jist enough poison to kill. Sometimes it don't use any poison. I'll tell you what. It makes you jump whenever it strikes at you."

Said, "We killed a bunch of 'em. But we knowed not to mess with one you shoot 'til the head's cut off, 'cause that thang can still strike you. Whenever you cut the head off, sometimes it looks like it's tryin' to strike you still."

Said, "Yeah, they do that. Have y'all been over there and seen the other animals?"

We said, "No."

Said, "Well, come over here and I'll take you." He took us in the back part. He introduced us to everybody and told 'em who we was and that Byron had jist won the shoot-off in the Okella National Forest. What a day! It jist got better all the time. We spent a couple of hours in the spring seein' the snake man, and then we left and got in the car.

I told Byron, I said, "I sure am tired."

He said, "Me too."

That man said, "Boys, you want a milkshake?" I never had 1 before. I'd heared of them though. That was somethin' rich kids had, not poor kids. Said, 'Ok."

So we went down and got us a milkshake. I drank every drop of that thang. I thought I was gonna explode. But boy! Was it good. It had them strawberries in it and all that stuff. And he told 'em to put extra cream in it so it tasted better.

We got back to Byron's house and he said, "Now boys, I'm gonna bring both of you a pistol, and I hope that you take an extra gun whenever you go after that snake. You take it in the boat and if you get in trouble you can shoot that snake in the face."

We looked up. Sure enough, he come back and he gave me a pistol. My brother wanted mine, so I give it to 'im. I didn't want mine. I had my .22 rifle.

The day had jist come to an end. It had been a great day. We'd been to everythin'. Byron was a champion. He had a big ole plaque that told 'im how good a shot he was. That man had got the rifle he wanted. We had a day like we'd never seen before. Only rich kids lived like that. We saw people's eyes bulge out whenever Byron'd nail that target every time or drive them nails. It was fun and we enjoyed every bit of it.

I come home and took my bath. I hadn't had 1 that day. And my mama said, "Supper will be ready in a little bit."

I said, "I don't need no supper. I need relief. I et too much today. I feel like I'm fixin' to explode."

She said, "What did you have?

I said, "We had barbecue, then we had a big ole steak at the steakhouse with the bull on top of it in Okella; then we went to Silver Springs and then he stopped and got us a milkshake at 1 of them places that makes milkshakes. It had big ole strawberries in that milkshake. It was so good. But I'm ready for bed." I went in there and rolled the covers back. After I layed down I don't remember nothin'.

I got up Sunday mornin' 'bout 7 o'clock. My dad was makin' breakfast. I put on my Sunday go-to-meetin' clothes and went to Sunday School and church. You'll never guess what the preacher preached on! Jonah and the Whale. I thought, *I jist wonder how big that whale would be.*

And they said, "It had to be huge if Jonah could live in 'im." I guess they was right.

We got out of church and Byron said, "You want to come to the house and eat lunch?"

I said, "No, I'm goin' home. I'm tired."

He said, "Boy, what a day we had yesterday. They won't ever be another one like it."

I said, "Nope. They sure won't. Them people know how good you are. And I'll tell you what, they won't let you shoot no more."

He said, "Well, they can't stop me if I pay my money."

I said, "You know what you got the most from? That time you shot the turkey. We done shot his money turkey!"

He said, "Yeah, we did, didn't we?"

"Well, I'll see you Monday at school."

He said, "Ok."

I walked down Main Avenue, crossed the track, walked in there and said, "Wow! What a day." I went in and lunch was ready. My mama had made some black-eyed peas and corn bread and cut off some ham and fried it. It was good. I had some water to drink. My mama washed the dishes up and my dad went out on the porch for his nap.

I went out in the barn and layed there; watched the rats and the snakes and the cat. It was fun to go there and lay in the peanut hay and eat the peanuts.We fed 'em to the mules. My dad said, "Don't eat all of 'em, 'cause the mules need some."

The next thang I knowed it was time for church again.

Yup, Back to the Woods

Chapter 45

I went to church and then walked the back way home. They was a big ole two-story buildin' that used to be the post office, but we still called it that. The big boys would get up in there on the second story and roll a 55-gallon drum across the floor. I was jist sure there was boogers in there. I warn't afraid of no snake, I warn't afraid of no gator, but I was afraid of them boogers 'cause you couldn't see 'em. They'd roll that drum, boom, boom, boom, boom; it scared the fire out of me.

I went on home. One day, I told Byron, I said, "We'll shoot that booger that's in there."

He said, "There ain't a booger in there; that's 1 of them older boys up there rollin' a drum around."

I said, "Oh." I didn't want 'im to know I was scared of it, but I was still scared.

The day ended like all the other days; it got dark and I washed my face and hands and feet and went to bed.

Monday mornin' we went back to school; same ole stuff. Everybody give up on the War of 1812, but there was other thangs. Somebody warn't payin' attention, and the teacher cracked 'im across the top of the head with a pencil. They always made a funny sound. "Thud."

School lasted all day that day and the next too. Then Friday, and nothin' had really happened that whole week. It had jist been 1 of them dull weeks. You did what you had to do. But Friday afternoon I told Byron, I said, "Byron, we need to get over there in them woods and see if we can see that ole snake."

He said, "Yeah, it's been a while since we been there."

"Yeah, we'll stop by Uncle Will's and see what he's got to say, first."

"Ok."

So Saturday mornin' I showed up at Byron's house 'bout 8 o'clock. He got his .45-70 and I had my .22 and we went up to see Uncle Will. He was sittin' out there buildin' a fire. It was a bit chilly. We said, "Uncle Will. What's goin' on?"

He said, "Well, I seen that ole Bill go down there in his cut-off truck and 'bout an hour later he come back."

Said, "Uh-oh." They ain't no tellin' what he's done. So we went down Stagecoach Road, went over to Cason Hammock, looked up, and he'd tore our ladder up that we'd climb up in the tree with. So we had to fix it. We got it fixed, and climbed up in the tree. He'd shot a hole through the floor in that thang and it had went through the tin roof and rained in there. It ruined our mattress we'd made of grass. It had molded, so we had to throw it out.

Byron said, "You know, I should have shot his big toe off when I had the chance."

I said, "No, it's like Uncle Will said, he's not all there in the head. He's a little empty in the brain." They had a piece of tin in the barn. So we tore the piece of tin off, went back by Byron's house. We got it and went back to put it on our place up in the tree. We got some feed sacks, but we didn't have no bed top grass. So we put them sacks up there and we could lie down. We nailed a board over the hole to keep the skeeters out.

He said, "Let's go down and see how our raft's doin' after that old ga-tor chewed the end off it." So we went down and guess what we found! Bill had drug our raft up on the bank, and it looked like he'd taken an axe and chopped it all in pieces. There warn't nothin' left we could fix.

Said, "That dirty ole rascal!"

I said, "I guess he was jist tryin' to get even with us for that tur-key-huntin' bit." Said, "We ain't through yet."

Byron said, "Well, we can shoot 'im."

Said, "That would put us in jail.We don't want to end up in jail."

Said, "Yeah." He said, "Let's go back to Uncle Will's and see what he's got to say.

He said, "Have you got any money?"

I said, "'Bout fifteen cents."

"Well, I got fifteen cents. Let's down to see if we can get Uncle Will some swamp water."

Said, "Ok." So we went over there and crossed that cable. We got over to Bugg Spring. We got on the other side, went there to where the shine place was at. They was still makin' shine; had 4 jars sittin' on each stump there. We dropped a quarter in there, 2 dimes and a nickel, and we had a nickel left. That'd get us a Black Cow candy bar. We come back across Bugg Spring Run, got to the other side and got our rifles and took the shine back toward Uncle Will's. Told Uncle Will, "We ain't been down there in the swamp yet; he may have tore that place down."

Uncle Will said, "You boys leave 'im alone. You know he ain't all there."

Said, "Yeah, we know, Uncle Will. But we tryin' to figure out somethin' we can do."

Said, "I know, boys. I had a man one time botherin' me like that and what I did was, I found me a big ole wasp nest and I took some splinters and burnt those wasps from the outside. They done capped off in there and the young ones was gonna hatch out. I put that thang under his bed and put a string around it, so if you pull that string the whole thang come out and all the wasps go out under his bed. I'm tellin' you boys, don't do that. There ain't no tellin' what that man would do."

Said, "Well, Uncle Will, you know we jist don't know what to do."

He said, "Well, don't do nothin', boys. You'll be better off."

We said, "Well, Uncle Will, we got you some swamp water."

He said, "Whew Doggie, boys! I sure is thirsty. I sure is thirsty. I want to thank you boys. Maybe I'll do somethin' for y'all someday."

We said, "You done do a lot for us, Uncle Will. We jist glad we can do it."

He said, "Y'all didn't steal the shine, did you?"

I said, "No, we bought it. We put two dimes and a nickel in the jar and got a pint of shine. I think that's what he gets."

Said, "That sounds 'bout right, that's 'bout right. You boys want a little swig?"

Said, "Nooo! I don't like that stuff. It burns."

Said, "Ok."

Said, "Well, we're goin' back down there and go to the swamp and see what's there."

Said, "You boys be careful in there. That's a bad place."

We told 'im, "Yeah, we know it is. We got to go."

He said, "Ok, y'all stop by when you come back, ok?"

So we went on down through the orange grove, looked for the snake tracks and couldn't see none. We went across the logs. Bill hadn't messed with that.We climbed up, layed up there for probably 'bout thirty minutes. Then Byron touched me and gave me the sign to be quiet. We layed there, and we seen the bushes shakin' a little bit. Guess what! A big old cat that we'd never saw before stepped out.

It was an ole bobcat. She stepped out with these little ole bitty cats behind her. They was followin' her along. Byron took his rifle and leveled it up and said, "I could kill her dead. But you know what, she ain't botherin' us, and all she is doin' is gettin' somethin' to eat. We ain't gonna mess with that."

We watched her for a second and then I don't know if she smelled us or what, but she bounced off through the woods. The kittens was right behind her. We layed there for another hour but didn't see nothin'. Kind of gettin' cloudy lookin', so Byron said, "We'd better get out of here.

We done lost our float, and we have to get us some more grass to put in them feed sacks.That ole Bill sure is bad news!"

Said, "We'll have to wasp nest 'im some day."

Said, "That'd be fine."

We went on back by Uncle Will's. He had layed his pipe down and we got us each a drag off the pipe and put it back down. We said, "Well, we're goin' on home, Uncle Will."

He said. "You boys be careful. You find anythin' else in there?"

We said, 'Yeah, he tore up our float and shot up a hole in the roof of our tree house. Byron said that he should have shot his toe off."

"No, no, don't do that. Y'all will get 'im one day."

So we went on back to Byron's house and I tell 'im, I said, "I'm goin' on home." So I went across the field and went over the fence and stopped at the house. Had to have my bath if I didn't want to suffer the consequences.

Sunday mornin' I went to Sunday School and church. Then I thought I'd jist go home. So I went home and my mama cooked up some quail that I'd caught down there in the trap. And she had some lima beans cooked and sweet taters and cat-eyed biskits. Boy! They's good. They was fluffy, and she shot them with jelly. My dad went out and layed on the porch and got 'im a nap. My mama layed on the bed and got her a nap. I went out to where the old hog was with her piggies, scratched her on the head and let her grunt and groan. She sure did like to be rubbed. I guess everybody likes to be rubbed though.

Come time to go back to church. I walked around that old two-story house. I was still scared of them boogers in it. Went out to the church. After church I said, "I'll see you in the mornin', Byron."

He said, "Ok."

We went to school Monday. Nothin' interestin' happened that day, nor on Tuesday, nor on Wednesday, and then on Thursday I said somethin' to Evelyn that she didn't like. She throwed me down in the dirt and rubbed my nose in that clay. I thought, *Well, I ain't sayin' that to her no more.*

I went in and washed my face off. She shook her finger at me. I knowed what she meant.

Mule Turns Green
for Halloween
Chapter 46

We left and come back down the sand road. We was jist shootin' the breeze like we do. And on Friday somebody got hit on the head with a pencil for not payin' attention again. Then on Saturday I went over to Byron's house. He said he had to rake the yard. So I helped 'im rake. We put the leaves out over in the clay road. A truck come by and the next thang you know, they'd all be gone.

We got all through rakin' 'em and went down to the hog pen where the swing was at. Byron's sister, Betty Jean, was down there. She said, "You know what? Halloween's next week."

I said, "It is?"

She said, "Yeah, it's the 31st of October next week."

I said, "Oh my goodness. Well, what are we gonna do for Halloween?"

Byron said, "I don't know."

I said, "Well, if we had us some dye, we could go over there and dye ole Henry's mule."

Betty Jean said, "What kind of dye you talkin' 'bout?"

Byron said, "There's clothin' dye, food dye, whatever kind we can get."

I said, "Byron, you got any money?"

He said, "I got a dollar, but that's all I got."

I said, "Why don't we go next Saturday and catch a ride to Leesburg and see what we can find."

So the week ended. Saturday we swung on the swing, milked the cow, went up and rubbed the ole mule. You take your thumb and reach under and stick 'im in the belly and he'll kick the barn door. That warn't much fun either, 'cause we was afraid he'd kick us. I decided I was gonna go home. I went across the field, went by the ole post office and on home. There was my mama, waitin'. Bath time! I tell you what, I'm beginnin' to believe that I have to take a bath every other day!

She said, "Well, it was last Saturday you had one. You need one now."

I said, "Well, I'll take it." They still made me take my bath last. So I took my bath and et my supper. We had black-eyed peas and corn bread with cracklins in it. Whew! Them thangs is good. They had little pieces of ham that she cooked on the stove and it was good too. We didn't have no ice tea since we didn't get no ice this week; jist didn't have the money. I et and went to bed. Slept like a log.

Got up Sunday mornin' and put my Sunday mornin' clothes on and went by Byron's before Sunday School and church. After church they had fried chicken. I got me a drumstick and et it. I stayed there a little while and then said, "I'm gonna go home."

So I went across the field, got home, piddled around for a couple of hours and then it was church time again.

Monday mornin' I got up, had breakfast 'bout 6 o'clock, went to school but nothin' excitin' happened. But they didn't bring up the War of 1812 no more. That was good.

My brother was cleanin' the buildin' up and he thought I should go up there and help 'im. He was gettin' money for it, but he didn't want to give me none. I didn't want to go up there.

Friday, Byron said, "Tomorrow, we goin' to town, aren't we?"

And I said, "Yeah, we goin' to town." So 'bout 11 o'clock we caught the train and took Betty Jean with us. We got off at the depot in Leesburg.

We walked down to the A&P Store on Main Street. We told 'em that we needed some dye.

They said, "What color?"

We said, "What color you got?"

He said, "Well, I got a bottle of dye here that I can't sell 'cause it's too big. It's food dye and it's green. If you buy it, I'll sell it to you for a dollar and a half. It's a full quart. It'll dye 'bout anythin'."

So we talked it over and decided to get it. That left us 25 cents. So we went ahead and bought the dye and decided we'd go down to Doc Carney's and get us some coke. He'd make coke down there. I don't remember what it was made of, but it was really good and it was different. He made us a coke and we gave 'im 15 cents. That left us with enough money to get us a can of Prince Albert and a Black Cow candy bar. We decided we'd catch the 4 o'clock freight. We'd never done that before. We knowed it would come and stop.

So we climbed in the box car and the train took off. We went all through the swamp down there, through the sawgrass curves and we was doin' good, me and Byron and Betty Jean. I heared the train whenever he blowed at the crossin', a long, a long, a short and a long. That meant a highball, so we warn't stoppin' in Okahumpka; we's goin' on. Well, he stopped down in Sumterville.We wasn't exactly sure where it was goin' to stop. Instead of bein' 5 miles from home, now we was 10 miles from home. There ain't nobody who travels on that Sumterville Hwy on Saturday, 'cause they all goin' to Sumterville, not leavin' it.

The foreman who did repairs on the highway lived in Okahumpka. When we got off the train he was walkin' on the track. He said, "What are y'all doin'?"

We said, "We're tryin' to get back home."

He said, "Well, get on here. I ain't supposed to let you ride on here, but get on." We rode up almost to South Quarter Road, and he said, "That's as far as I'll take you; y'all have to get out and walk the rest of the way."

So we got off and walked down the road. We still had our quart of food dye. Byron said, "Next Friday night, we gonna take and dye that ole mule."

Said, "Ok, we'll do it. I'll tell my mama I'm gonna spend the night with you. And you tell your mama you're gonna spend the night with me, and Betty Jean should come spend the night too.

He said, "Ok."

All week long we were lookin' forward to this. We got us some old socks to put on our hands. We warn't exactly sure how good this dye was goin' to be. So Friday afternoon, Byron's little brother, Larry, walked by. He was gonna be our guinea pig. Said, "Larry, come here. Let's make your arms green."

So we dyed his arms, and they turned green. He liked it. He said he had the only green arms in the neighborhood.

We said, "Well, that's purty good."

Byron said, "We ought to dye 'im all over."

I said, "I don't know 'bout that, Byron. I don't know what your mama will say when she sees that."

He said, "Aw, she won't say nothin'." But we didn't do it.

That night, 'bout 7 o'clock we eased through the woods, went down the road, and ole Henry's donkey brayed when we walked out on the field where he was. He was as friendly as could be; he was a good ole mule. We took that quart of food dye and we dyed that ole white mule green. And I mean, he was green! Green! Well, no bad thang 'bout that. He looked purty good. Jist looked green.

So we decided we'd used up all the dye, so we went back through the grove and took the old socks and threw 'em away. The next mornin', I had a green arm! So we decided what we'd do; we'd go to the spring over there and get that sand and take some of the lye soap they made and was gonna scrub it off. Betty Jean wanted to go too.

We got over there and stripped off our clothes and waded over in the spring. We scrubbed and we scrubbed and we got that soap and we tried every way in the world to get that green dye off us. It jist wouldn't come off. So we both had one green arm. Larry had two! I went home and my mama said, "What have you been into?"

I said, "Food dye."

She jist said, "Well, what will you do next?"

I said, "I'm not sure, but I can't get it off."

So she told me I might try a bit of vinegar on it. It might help. Well, it helped a little but they was still green. Sunday we got up and went to church with our green arms.

I said, "Byron, what did your mama say?"

He said, "She whipped me and Betty Jean both. If you had been there you would have got it too."

I said, "I'm glad I warn't there. My mama tried to help me get it off." Have you seen the mule?"

"No, I ain't seen 'im."

He said, "Henry come over to the house and said that he wanted to see them boys that done it."

"Oh, dear. I wonder what's gonna happen out of this."

He said, "My mama whipped my behind for Larry havin' green arms. I ain't gonna say nothin'."

Well, my dad come in from work. I looked up and there was Henry. *Uh-oh.* I thought, *Goodness, what in the world is gonna happen next?*

My dad said, "Boy, did you take and put that stuff on ole Henry's mule over yonder and turn it green?"

I said, "Yes, sir, I did."

He said, "It looks good, but he's a little upset 'bout it. So whenever you get in from school Monday, I want you to get a bucket and one of them brushes and some lye soap and go over there and scrub that stuff off."

I said, "Ok."

He said, "It'll probably take you 3 days to get all that stuff off. Don't bother to take it off his head, that'll wear off eventually."

I told 'im, "Ok."

I started across the field and saw Byron and Betty Jean comin'. They had done got talked to too. We looked out there and we all were laughin. That was the greenest mule you ever seen. He looked purty though. I'd of left 'im green if he was mine.

So Henry come out there and says, "Boys what in the world possessed you to take and dye my mule green?"

We said, "Well, he looked like he needed it."

"Well, y'all gonna scrub it off, right?"

"Yeah, we gonna scrub it off."

Well, Henry went back to the house and his wife come out. She thought it was so funny she didn't know what to do. And I think that's the reason Henry got so mad 'bout it, 'cause she was laughin' so much.

She said, "I got this ole mule and he looks purty now!"

Well, we found out he'd try to kick us, so we tied his front legs and his back legs on both sides. He can't kick you with that done. If he kicks you, you fall down, so we didn't want to try it without the ropes. We rubbed 'im and he liked that. He rolled his skin and everythin'.

That green come off purty good. He still had some spots on 'im that we couldn't get though. We washed 'im all down.We had to pump the water and with each bucket if we looked like we were startin' to leave, Henry would come out and say, "Now, boys, don't come and take my ole mule again. Everybody in the neighborhood has been laughin' 'bout it. If they hain't been laughin', it wouldn't have been so bad. But they laughin' 'bout it, and I guess it is kind of funny. Next time, do somethin' to someone else's mule."

I said, "I don't think we'll do somebody else's. We jist had to do somethin' for Halloween."

He said, "Well, you had to pay for it. And that's fine." He said, "By the way, where'd you get that dye?"

We said, "We spent our last two dollars on it."

"Two dollars? Good gracious. If you'd have give me 1 of them dollars, I wouldn't have made you take the green off."

We said, "We didn't know that. We didn't have another dollar."

We left there through the orange grove.

Byron said, "You know what, let's go to the spring and wash up."

Said, "Ok, we can do that."

We cut across, went to the spring, went across the grove and there it was—that ole snake track again!! He's travelin' again. Said, "He's stayin' away from Uncle Will's place. He's not runnin' like he was."

We was goin' over by Uncle Will's and through that grove and the pasture, so he's goin' towards Lake Denham. He might be out on that island. So we'll take our boat and we'll go out there and see if he's there.

We go to the spring and shucked our clothes and washed off the dirt and scrubbed the dye off. We cleaned up purty good. We got back and put our clothes on and walked back through the grove.

We stopped by Uncle Will's to tell 'im what we done. Betty Jean was with us.

He said, "Yeah, everybody knows 'bout that green mule." He said, "What made you boys do that?"

We said, "Well, Uncle Will, there warn't nothin' else to do, so we decided we'd do that."

He layed down his pipe and we got a drag off it. Betty Jean took a drag too. We layed it back down and said, "Uncle Will, we'll see you in a day or two. We're still tryin' to figure out what to do with ole Bill." Said, "We'll shoot 'im is what we ought to do."

He said, "No, boys, you need to leave that ole Bill alone. He ain't nothin' but trouble."

He asked Betty Jean if she'd like to see his little goat. He walked up to the pen and pulled some grass up and fed 'em. They'd eat the grass. I told Uncle Will, I said, "You gonna cook and eat them goats?"

He said, "Yeah, one day I might do it, but right now, I'm not gonna do anythin' with them goats." Said, "What you gonna do the rest of the week now? You done got in trouble over there with that man. They gonna put you in jail."

Said, "If'n we went to jail, somebody'd come get us out."

He said, 'I ain't got no money to get you out of jail. They ain't gonna let a black man like this go in there and let 2 white boys out of jail."

I said, "Uncle Will, we jist did it 'cause if we got put in jail, you'd sell them goats or somethin' to get us out of jail. We'd appreciate that.We ain't really done nothin' that bad to get us in jail for though. 'Cause that ole man with the mule said if people hadn't have laughed 'bout it so much, he wouldn't have done nothin'."

He said, "Yeah, I guess so. You boys need to slow down a little bit, with everythin'. Even that ole snake scared of you."

I said, "Nah, he ain't scared of us, Uncle Will."

Byron said, "Are y'all ready to go?

"Yeah."

So we went and crossed the marsh and swung on the swing. Jerry, Byron's brother, was there in the hog pen foolin' with the hogs. So we got by the house and I said, "I'm goin' home. It's Saturday and you know what happens on Saturday! I have to take a bath." So I went across the field and climbed the fence, went by the spooky house and went on home. My mama told me to take a bath. I told her that I bathed over yonder but she said, "I don't care if you bathed over yonder, you gonna take a bath."

I jist said, "Yes, ma'm."

And wouldn't you know it, she had that bottle of castor oil and the big ole spoon. I really didn't want to take none of that stuff. I took my bath,et supper, sat around for a little while, sat by the fireplace, crawled into my feather bed and curled up. I was warm as toast in a few minutes and went to sleep. 'Bout 11 o'clock my brother come in and put his cold feet on me again! I'll get even with 'im some day for that.

The next mornin' was church time. After church I come home and et and then went out there where the sow was layin'. She was tryin' to scratch her side, so I scratched it for her. She was gruntin' and groanin'. Them little piggies liked it too. They gained 'bout 30-40 pounds now. They didn't know it, but their heyday was comin' to an end. Whenever it got good and cold, we'd butcher 'em up.

Went to school the next week with nothin' excitin' happenin'. On Friday, Byron said, "Let's go down there and get in the boat and go on Lake Denham."

Redskins, Pokeweed Tribe

Chapter 47

I said, "That'd be good."

So Saturday mornin' 'bout 8 o'clock I was at Byron's house with my .22 and he had his .45-70. We took off over there and climbed the pen and got into our tree house. It hadn't leaked any since we'd stuck that piece of tin on it.

We layed up there for a couple hours but all we saw was a black snake come by. There warn't no other varmints in the woods that day, that we could see. We thought maybe the snake was on the island. I said, "Ok. If you will oar us out to Lake Denham, I'll oar us to the island. If that snake's there, you can blow his head off. He won't sink."

He said, "Ok, we'll do that."

So we climbed out of the tree stand and layed our rifles in the boat. We didn't load 'em' cause it's dangerous to load a rifle in a boat. We looked and guess what we saw! Ole Bill had shot a hole in the bottom of our boat!! Byron said, "I knowed I should have shot 'im!"

So I said, "Let's turn the boat over and see what we can do."

We turned the boat over and we got the nails out of that 1 board. I said, "I'm gonna take this home and see if I can get my daddy to cut me a board to fix this thang."

So I come back home and Byron stopped at his house. I come home and asked my dad if he'd saw me a board shaped like that, 'cause Bill had shot a hole in the board. He said, "What's ole Bill doin' over there anyway?"

I said, "I don't know, but Bill does."

Said, "Ok."

It took 'im a whole weekend. He needed to heat the tin up and go to the little fire. Then put tar around the edges and then galvanized the nails in it. You can't put regular nails in it 'cause they'll rot and the board will fall off. He said, "You might have to put the board in the water for a bit, let it swell up. Don't put the tar real heavy, put it light."

So I went back by Byron's house. He was there. I had the nails and the board. We had our rifles with us. We went back over and walked by the tree house on down by the burnt-out stumps. We put the board on the boat and it fit. We had to do a little sandin' on the edges to smooth it. Then we put it in the water. It leaked a little bit but we had a coffee can we could dip the water out with. Byron oared the boat up to Helena Run and then headed toward Lake Denham. He got in the front of the boat and I oared.

We got to the island, but there warn't nothin' there but an ole moccasin. I shot it with my .22. It was purty quiet on the lake that day. We looked for tracks of the big snake where it might have crawled through the sawgrass, but we didn't see nothin'. We jist figured he warn't around.

It was gettin' to be 'bout noon time, so we oared back down, had to dip water out of the boat and then said, "Why don't we leave this thang sittin' in the water, so it will swell up better?"

"Ok, we can do that." We come back over and climbed into the tree house, 'cause we had some salt bacon up there. It keeps real good. We got our fryin' pan out and built us a little fire. We fried us up some bacon and et that for our lunch. I said, "You know what? Them Injuns, they go through the woods and nobody can see 'em or hear 'em. 'Cause of their red skins."

Byron said, "Let's go over yonder and pick us some of them poke-berries."

I said, "We tried that once before but it didn't last."

He said, "Let's try it again. We'll boil them thangs. Then we'll take and put a little bit on to see how it works."

I said, "Sounds fine to me." So we went over to Byron's and got us a bucket. We went to the west side of Lake Denham swamp where there was a bunch of 'em pokeberry bushes. Doves come in there and they eat 'em and the foxes and the coons eat 'em. Everybody but us, cause we was afraid to eat pokeberries. We was scared they was poison. They's red and some say, "Don't eat nothin' red."

We got to Byron's house again and boiled them thangs down in a pan. It was a little bit sticky but it was still pliable. We was talkin' 'bout who was gonna be first, and then Larry walked by. He got green arms; why not a red face?

"Yeah."

So we say, "Larry, wanna be an Injun?"

He said, "Yeah!"

We said, "Well, go get your headdress and come down here."

He come back with his headdress on, and Byron said, "Here, let me put this red stuff on your face so you look like an Injun."

He said, "Ok."

Byron rubbed it on his face; it looked purty good. So I got me a handful and rubbed it on my face and arms and they turned red. Byron then put it on 'im too. We even got Betty Jean in it. We said, "We'll jist put it on your hand." Well, she couldn't wash it off.

We were red-skinned men, so we decided we'd go back over to the swamp. We went by Uncle Will's. He was sittin' out underneath that tree. He said, "Boys! What in the world is wrong with y'all?"

We said, "Nothin'."

He said, "Your face is red as fire."

We said, "We Injuns."

He said, "What?"

We said, "We Injuns. We put red berries on us, and we Injuns."

He said, "I don't know what you is, but when you get home, your mama gonna beat your butt."

I said, "Naw, she don't care."

Said, "Yeah, don't tell her I told you to put any of that on your face."

We said, "They ain't nothin' to it."

He said, "Yeah, they is somethin' to it, boys. I bet your mama will put the switch on your behind like you ain't never had it before."

I said, "Aw, she won't be mad."

He said, "Ok."

So we left Uncle Will's and crossed the field and went down the dirt

road. Instead of goin' to the right we went to the left and we walked on
down almost to the spring. But we didn't go in 'cause we wanted this
pokeberry stuff to dry.

I said, "I don't feel so good though, I feel like it's crawlin' up."

Byron said, "Maybe we should go wash this stuff off."

So we went down and took our clothes off and climbed in the
spring. The water was cold. We washed and left some red-lookin' stuff
in the water.

He said, "Well, it all come off, didn't it?"

And I said, "Uh-uh. You still red as fire."

"I am?"

"Yeah, you are! I'm red, too. You an Injun now."

He said, "I'm an Injun?"

I said, "You an Injun."

He said, "Oh, that's alright." So we got back out and put our clothes
on. We went back to the grove. We didn't see no snake tracks. We went
across the logs into the Lake Denham swamp and climbed up on the
board there. Bill had shot a hole in that too. They warn't no damage
though, jist a hole in the board. We layed up there for a couple of hours.
A couple of gators swam by in the canal. They warn't very big. Byron
said, "We could shoot 'im."

I said, "Yeah, but I don't want to clean 'im."

He said, "Yeah, we could sell the hide though."

I said, "I don't want to clean 'im."

So we didn't shoot 'im. We let 'im go 'cause he was too much work.
Then a boar hog come by in a little bit. He swam down through the
canal. A coon come by in a little bit. It went to the water to wash its
hands. They were some squirrels. So we decided to shoot us a couple
of 'em and go and cook 'em on an open fire. We shot two squirrels, cut
'em across the back and skinned them out. We climbed down out of the
stand and went across the logs again down through the hammocks. We
went to Cason Hammock and built us a fire. We got some salt and pepper to put on them and cooked them fellas up. They was good. Byron et
one and I et one.

He said, "Let's walk down and see how our boat's doin', see if it's
swelled any." It had 'bout an inch of water in it, which is alright.

Byron said, "Why don't we drag it up on the bank?" So we drug the boat up on the bank and left the water in it. We can always get it out. We turned around and left and went back to our tree house. We climbed up in there and layed down on our grass beds that Uncle Will had layed out for us. We was layin' there, and sure enough, here it comes!

We knowed it warn't the snake though; we knowed it must be that old hog again. We'd tried shootin' through his ears and thought he would learn, but it seemed like he didn't. He walked on out. It was a little old sow, weighed 'bout 25-30 pounds.

We said, "Want to eat 'im?"

I said, "Yeah, I will. Kill 'im."

He said, "You gonna clean it?"

I said, 'Yeah, I'll clean it. Shoot 'im in the head, that way you won't waste nothin'. We'll go back to Uncle Will's and we'll skin 'im out there."

He said, "That'll be fine."

We shot the hog, got us a pole and carried 'im between us, our rifle and our hog. We carried it up to Uncle Will's house. He was sittin' up there under his tin shed makin' a fire there. It warn't cold, but it was chilly.

We brought the hog up and I skinned 'im. Uncle Will cut the feet off and the front part off and cut the tender part out of the back. He gave that to me and Byron. We'd cut it in half and bring it home.

My mama cooked mine. I don't know what Byron's mama done with his, but I'm sure she cooked it, cause that's the best part of the hog.

Uncle Will cooked those others up. He didn't have no 'frigerator, so he couldn't keep it unless he cooked it. He'd cook it and we'd eat off it the whole week. I gave the pork chop that I had to my mama and she cooked it for supper that night.

It was a long day. We'd been mad at ole Bill, who shot our tree house, he shot our boat, and he shot everythin' we had. Maybe we ought to shoot 'im and shoot his ole car. But I thought, *No, they'd put us in jail for that. What we'd need to do is put them wasp nests up underneath his feetee and up underneath his bed.*

The day ended. Like all Saturdays, I had to take a bath, even though I already had 1 in that spring. It's a beautiful spring over there. All trees, the water 'bout 2 foot deep and cool as can be. All you got to do is watch for snakes in the trees around there. We killed a bunch of 'em, but they always come back to cool places. Snakes like warm weather and them moccasins will swim in anythin'.

So I took my bath and et my supper. I et a piece of that ole hog. We took the skin and saved it 'cause we decided we was gonna put it on the stump over there, and maybe somethin' would come around and we could kill it too. But if we can't eat it or skin it, we don't kill it.

Sunday mornin' come around and I got my Sunday clothes on. I put my shoes on. Boy! they was cold. They'd built a fire in the woodstove in the church. Everybody'd gather round and the preacher get up and preached the sermon. I don't remember what he preached on, but it was probably 'bout us. Everybody knowed that we'd been in everythin'.

We got through with church and Byron asked if I wanted to come over to the house. I told 'im, "No, I'm goin' home."

I went back home, took my Sunday clothes off and put my other clothes on and went out to visit the pigs again. They's 'bout 70-80 pounds now. That's a really good size. My mother called 'em "boar hogs."

It was gettin' late in the afternoon and gettin' darker every day. I went back to church that night, walked by that old depot and then went by the booger house. The man that owned it, or said he did, turned out he didn't; he said that the mess around the thang was bad.

I was tired and went home and went to bed. I didn't even wash my face, my feet or my hands. I jist went to bed. It'd been a long week.

I got up Monday mornin'. My daddy had gotten up and fixed breakfast. He got me up 'bout 6:30. I had my 2 eggs and my grits and I was sittin' there eatin' them.

He said, "Boy, what happened to your face?"

I said, "What do you mean?"

He said, "Your face and your arms are red as fire."

I said, "Oh, we went over there and got us some pokeberries. We was gonna be Injuns, since them Injuns can go in the woods and nobody sees them or nothin'. And we were gonna kill that snake. We figured if he couldn't see or hear us, well, then we'd have a better chance of killin' 'im."

He said, "Does that mess wash off?"

I said, "No, it don't wash off."

He said, "Well, you sure are a red-faced Injun. You got red hair too.

You ought to dye your hair black. The Injuns don't have red hair."

I said, "Oh, you mean they gonna be able to see my red hair?"

He said, "That's right." He said, "But I'd leave it red. It won't hurt nothin.'"

Well, we went on to school. We showed up and was sittin' on them steps. I said, "Byron, what did your mama say 'bout your red face?"

He said, "She whipped my behind."

"She did?"

He said, "Yeah, look at Larry. He's got green arms and a red face."

I said, "She jist whipped you?"

He said, "Yes. And when I did it again, she'd put a beatin' on me. She whipped Betty Jean too. She thought Betty Jean was involved in it. Her hands was red, so she knowed she helped."

He said, "What did your mama say?"

I said, "She said nothin.' My dad did. He said, 'It ain't gonna do no good to put my face red and leave my hair red.'"

My dad said, "Well, you ain't no Injun and you won't never be an Injun."

I said, "Yeah, but we gotta kill that snake. We don't want 'im to see us."

Dad said, "You gonna have to do it different. That's all I can tell you."

I said, 'Oh, ok."

"Have you seen 'im lately?"

"We haven't seen 'im lately, but we've seen his tracks.

He said, "You may have to put somethin' out there, so he'll come out and eat it. Somethin' like 1 of them ole roosters or somethin' like that. Put a rope around his leg and bring 'im out somewhere so he can't get out, like around that stump."

"Hmm. We can try that, but there's gators over there and there's coons. They'll all try to eat 'im up and they'll let 'im loose."

He said, "Oh, you can't lose 'im."

I said, "So I guess I got away with havin' a red face. What does Larry think 'bout his face and arms?

Byron said, "He don't care. He had green arms, now he's a red face Injun. He's all in one, so he's happy."

I said, "Has he tried to get the green off?"

He said, 'No, he don't want to touch it. He don't want to wash it off his face either. But he said it felt funny; it tingles."

I said, "Hmm."

"Well, I don't think we'd better do that again. My mama really tore my behind up. She got her a switch and she worked on me and she worked on Betty Jean. We was screamin' and hollerin'. Too late to worry 'bout that now."

We walked into school and headed into the class room. The teacher looked at Byron and said, "What's wrong with you?"

He said, "I'm an Injun."

She said, "You're a what?"

He said, "I'm an Injun. A red-faced Injun."

She said, "You mean Indian?"

"Yes."

"Well, what's wrong with y'all?"

"We're Injuns."

"Your face always that red?"

"When we put pokeberries on it, yes."

We was full-blooded Injuns. We'd seen 'em on those cowboy shows at the movies when we could go. And we wanted to be like one of 'em. We killed a bunch of rattle snakes, and them Injuns done that, too. We hadn't shot any cowboys. We'd like to shoot ole Bill. It looked fun. I don't know if I'd put that on my face again, though, 'cause I didn't know if it would ever come off. I might be a red-faced Injun all my life. But I doubt it.

Well, school let out late out that day. There warn't nothin' excitin' goin' on. Then I walked down the road and went home, washed my face and washed my hands and washed my feet.

I et my supper and went to bed. It was kind of chilly outside but the bed was warm. It had that feather mattress on it. You jist lay in that thang and you ball up and soon you'll be as warm as toast. 'Course my brother comes in 'bout 11 o'clock and sticks his ole cold feet on me. But I'd had a good day and a good week.

Never Give Up

Chapter 48

The whole week was 'bout the same. Somebody didn't pay attention again and got rapped on the head with a pencil or a ruler! Friday, Byron said, "What are we gonna do tomorrow?"

I said, "I don't know."

He said, "We have to go over to that swamp and see if we can kill that snake. We jist need to kill 'im. Maybe on the inside of that hog we left over there, maybe somethin' come over there to eat it and the snake's there."

I said, "Ok. I'll be over there Saturday mornin' 'bout 8 o'clock."

I took me two of them wrappers off the bread. I saved 'em. And I put 'em over my feeet so that whenever I waded in on the Cypress logs they wouldn't get too wet. If your feet don't get wet, you don't get as cold. We waded in and climbed up on the platform. The wind was blowin' purty good and it were cold up there.

We said, "Let's go over to the tree house. We can stay in that better." So we went over to the tree house; climbed up in the there and stayed there. We layed there for a good hour. The tree house had good wind breaks on it. We had stuff we could stick up on the sides to keep the wind off. We didn't see nothin' important come by. We saw an old sow come by with a bunch of little pigs. We thought we would get one of 'em some day, but they was too little now.

We heared somethin' comin' and knowed it was that snake!

I said, "Look there. You see them bushes shaking?" So Byron got his .45-70, got it all cocked back. Then the shakin' stopped. We sat there and waited. It seemed like a long time, but you know what? It jist stopped.

Byron said, "You know what? That snake knows we're up in this tree! When he sticks his head out, I'm gonna blow it off!"

Well, when he stuck his head up, it was that ole boar hog again! Really, he don't do us no harm, so we ain't gonna shoot 'im. We done shot holes in his ears already. They looked kinda bad, like they was infected or somethin' But, I don't guess he minds too much. He jist buried up in the mud. He smelled bad too. If we'd shot 'im he'd stunk the whole place up.

So we let 'im go on by and we layed up there. It looked like it was gettin' dark, and I said, "Let's go home." We climbed down out of the tree house, went over to Stagecoach Road and went behind Uncle Will's house. He had a little fire goin', so we warmed our hands and feet a bit. He cut us off a piece of the ole ham and we et it. Then he said, "I ain't seen that ole snake come by here in a long time. He must be movin' on."

"No, we saw 'im movin' through the grove 'bout a month ago. And last week he was on that island. I think what he's done is, he's gone across the lake over there 'cause he knows we're chasin' 'im."

He said, "Could be."

Byron said, "We don't want to go set up a platform over there 'cause we don't know them people over there, and ain't no tellin' what they'll do to us if they catch us up there."

He said, "You're right, boys. You're right. You know, your face is still red. Yes, it is."

I said, "My mama scrubbed mine with some of the lye soap and it still didn't come off. So I guess we Injuns. We probably be Injuns all our life."

He said, "Naw, it'll wash off some day."

Byron said, "My little brother has it too. But he likes it. He's got green arms and a red face!"

Uncle Will said, "He likes it?"

"Oh, yeah, he likes it."

He asked Byron, he said, "What'd your mama say 'bout that?" Byron said, "She beat the fire out of me! She told me if I done somethin' like that again, she would really put a whippin' on me. She even whipped my sister, 'cause she had red hands. She'd been in them pokeberries with her hands."

Uncle Will said to me, "What you' mama say to you 'bout it?"

I said, "She didn't say nothin'. My daddy laughed 'bout it. He said he didn't really care."

We said, "Well, we'll see ya, Uncle Will. We're fixin' to go home."

We took a drag off his pipe and we waded through the marsh. That water was cold. We went behind the cow pen and behind Byron's house. I went across the field to home. I still had to take my bath. They had a fire in the fireplace. The fire got so hot on 1 side you'd burn you ole nekkid behind. We et supper and went to bed. I was tired.

 Tomorrow's another day.

I got up Sunday mornin', put on my Sunday clothes and went to church. It was a little bit chilly, not bad; but it was in the forties. They'd done built a fire in that ole stove. Preacher preached the sermon, probably 'bout Byron and me. Then I walked on home. I really didn't want to go nowhere. I wanted to go out and see that ole sow and her pigs. I liked goin' out there and watchin' 'em.

We had lunch, but I don't 'member what we et. They's always some ole biskits. You can't make any better biskits than lard biskits. My dad layed on the porch and took a nap and my mama layed on the bed. I went to see the pigs. I caught me one and that ole sow looked at me kind of funny, didn't say much, but her baby was squealing. So I scratched 'im on the belly and he shut up. They all liked to be scratched on the belly. I played out there with them pigs for a while, then come in and washed my hands, 'cause they was real muddy.

It was time to go back to church. I went in and put my Sunday clothes back on and went back to church. I went to BYPU. Know what that stands for? "Buy Your Preacher's Underwear." It warn't what they said it meant; it was somethin' else. It was like "Sunday School" but a little bit different. The preacher got up and preached a sermon. They had 1 light in the church and it had a pull cord, not a switch.

After church I come on home. I didn't want to walk by that ole two-story buildin' with the boogers in it. I knowed it had boogers. I heared 'em up in them rafters too many times to say there ain't no boogers in it. I got home and didn't even wash my feete or my hands or my face. I didn't get dirty that day. I ain't been in nothin' all day.

Good Duck Huntin'

Chapter 49

I got up the next mornin' 'bout 6 o'clock, had my grits and eggs. My daddy had them biskits made. Sometimes he'd fire up some of that bacon. I loved that-there bacon. Sometimes he'd get some of them sausages out he'd made and he'd cook 'em. We et breakfast. We don't have to go to school; the teachers were havin' a day for somethin' else. My daddy said, "I don't want you to go to school Friday. I want you to go to the field with me."

I said, "Ok, I can do that." I always liked to go to the field with 'im. They was always somethin' different 'bout it. He raised all them vegetables to sell.

Thursday, Byron said, "What you gonna do tomorrow?"

I said, "I'm goin' to work with my dad. I can't meet you tomorrow. But Saturday mornin', if you want to, we'll go over back to that hammock and see if we can catch that snake."

Well, Friday mornin' we got up 'bout 6 o'clock and et breakfast. We got started early.

We was goin' down the road and I told 'im, "Stop". I saw somethin'. He said, "What'd you see?"

I said, "I saw one of 'em little gators. I'm gonna catch that gator." I got out of the truck, but he'd already run out there into the swamp. I didn't want to go get 'im 'cause a mama gator might be around, and

I didn't need to be out there fiddlin' around the pond with a mama gator. We went on to the field. We went down to the creek and went by Pepper Lake. We was farmin' out on the hill. He gave me a box of .22 bullet and said, "Kill all the fox squirrels and all the gophers and all the rattlesnakes you see."

I said, "Ok."

He said, "Be careful out there."

I said, "Ok."

So I ran through the woods and I come up on the creek over there and I heared these ducks. So I decided what I'd do is crawl on down there and see if I could shoot 'em. I crawled on there, but then this old cottonmouth moccasin swam right in front of me. I thought, *If'n I shoot that moccasin, them ducks is gonna fly. If I let 'im go by, it's alright.*

So I crawl on down the where the ducks is at. I was 'bout 20 feet from 'em; they was 'bout 10-15 in that bunch. They was bobbin' down eatin'. I thought, *When 1 of them comes up, I'll shoot 'im in the head.* One of 'em popped up and I popped 'im in the head. I made sure that bullet didn't hit the water and scare the rest of them ducks.

I shot 4 of 'em that way; then all of a sudden 2 of them come up at one time. They smelled them dead ducks, and they jumped up and flew. I didn't shoot em' then. I warn't that good. Now, if Byron was along he would have shot 'em.

And then there was that ole moccasin. I tell you he was watchin' them ducks too. I don't know why he was watchin' 'em; he couldn't have swallowed 1 down, but he might have. I looked over the side of 'im and there was an ole gator easin' toward 'im. I ricochateed a bullet off that ole gator's head, and he lit out through the sawgrass jist to get away. It probably shook 'im up a little bit. I didn't want to kill 'im 'cause I didn't want to skin 'im.

I looked over there and there was that ole moccasin lookin'. I shot 'im upside the head. He was a big ole moccasin, not long, but big. He was a black cottonmouth. I waded out there and got them ducks and went back to the truck. I picked the wings off 'em, 'cause there ain't much on the wing of a duck, and I put them feathers and down off 'em in one of them sacks we had behind the seat. My mama would take and make feather pillows out of 'em. She'd cut them stubby ends off. I took all the feathers I could pick off and pulled all the pin feathers out. Then I built me a fire and singed all the rest of the hair off that I could get. I took all the guts out and saved all the gizzards. I cleaned 'em and made sure they didn't have nothin' on 'em. They're good.

I took 'em down and put 'em in that hole where we put our water every day. My daddy'd take this piece of stainless steel pipe and dig it down next to the pond. He'd put his water in it and that would keep the water cool all day. It wouldn't be like puttin' it on ice, but it would be a lot better than takin' and jist leavin' it out.

So I eased on down to the field there when I heared that ole buzz tail sound. I said, "Yup, it's there somewhere." And there it was, a diamond-back. I shot it and thought, *They's another one 'round where they's one at.* So I threw a stick over in the meadows. Yup, it was a heartback. I'd got the male and the female both. I shot the female and looked and there was a little ole rattlesnake there. He warn't more than 4 inches long. So I got me a stick and put it over in the pile.

Okahumpka Methodist Chapel.

Who's Chasin' Who?

Chapter 50

It's another Saturday, so we went behind the house. Byron had his .45-70 and I had my .22. We went down and sat there with Uncle Will a little bit. He warn't feelin' too good. He was kind of under the weather a little bit. He wanted to know if we could go get 'im another bottle of that wine. He called it "wine", but it warn't nothin' but homemade wiskey. The still was over in them-there woods, and they was makin' that wiskey.

We said, "Yeah, we'd get it." We had a quarter on us, between us. We was 'bout 3 cents short, but I said that man wouldn't care, as long as we put it all in there at some point. Then we went down to Spring Run. We took one of them glass jars with us and set it down. We put the money in the can. Like I say, we was 3 cents short, so we left 'im a note that said, "IOU 3 cents," and we'd get it for 'im.

Then we left, but we stopped and watched the man. He went over there and picked up the can to count the change. He looked over to where we was, and I thought, *Hmm, he ain't happy 'bout that. We done cheated 'im out of three cents*. But we'd give 'im his 3 cents later. Uncle Will was honest and we was too.

We went back towards our tree house, but there warn't nothin' there. We have our rifles with us; we wouldn't go into them woods without no rifle. We went down Stagecoach Road and back down the trail. Uncle

Will was sittin' there. He didn't look like he felt good either. So we gave 'im his bottle. He said, "Boys, I thank you. I'll get your quarter back to you one day."

We said, "We was 3 cents short, but we'll get it to 'im one day."

He said, "That's fine."

We decided we'd go back over to the hammock, so we went over and climbed back up in our tree house. They warn't much goin' on; no noise; no nothin'. So we went back over to Lake Denham Swamp. It was gettin' kinda chilly and kinda cold. We waded across to the tree and put our rifles up against the tree. I climbed up almost to where the top of the platform was at and I hollered, "Byron, Byron, get up here quick." He scrambled up the tree and that big snake was right behind 'im. He almost caught 'im. I thought, *Boy, here we are; we almost caught 'im and all we got up here is a hammer!*

I said, "I hope them rattlesnakes don't climb trees. I never heared of one of 'em climbin' a tree." But there he was on the ground and he was lookin' at us. He knowed where we was at; he knowed we didn't have no gun. That snake's smart!!

We realized we was in trouble, but we got to talkin' 'bout this thang. Whenever we was in the grove, I bet that snake were in that grove. He followed us in there. We didn't hear 'im come in there, but we was thinkin' he followed us. He must of been chasin' us the whole time.

We'd made a mistake of leavin' our guns on the ground. We won't make that mistake no more. We gonna get us a rope where we can pull our guns up. And when we go up the tree we'll hook 'em guns on that rope. We'll get 'em up there so he can't trap us no more. But it's too late to worry 'bout that now. We'd done gotten ourselves into a mess.

It was gettin' a little bit chilly, and we may be up here all night. If'n we have to stay, we jist have to stay. We ain't gonna get down there with no rattlesnake and fight 'im with a hammer. His fangs is like 16-penny nails. If he hit you, it'd go all the way through you. And that's the end of you.

But ole Joe gator swam by and we said somethin's goin' to have to happen around this place before we get in real trouble. And we was already in real trouble. Uncle Will told us not to come down here in these woods, and he's probably right!

But we still ain't give up on this snake. We gonna get that thang. He's down there lookin' at us and we're up here lookin' at 'im. Byron said, "Throw the hammer at 'im."

I said, "No, I ain't gonna throw this hammer at 'im."

He said, "Why not?"

I said, "That's the only thang we got up here to fight 'im with. We can't spit on 'im. We gonna have to keep this hammer up here."

The sun was lurkin' in the clouds a little bit. But it got a little more chilly. I said, "I'm cold!"

He said, "Me too."

I said, "I got my feet wet and my feet are freezing on me." It had done got down to probably 50 or 60 degrees. I said, "I thought snakes can't stand cold temperatures."

He said, "No regular snake down there." Said, "That thang's a monster."

Well, we looked down at 'im and sure enough, he looked back at us. You could see his eyes. They gleamed. We noticed it was comin' a rain cloud back on the west of us. And the more we watched that cloud the more we thought we was fixin' to get some wind and rain. All of a sudden lightnin' struck over there on the other side of the lake.

Said, "Hmm. I hope there don't come lightnin' storm in here."

Then it happened. Lightnin' struck that pine tree next to where we was at. It shocked us. Our hair stood straight up! Ole Joe, the gator, he took off through the sawgrass, and the snake, he run west. Byron jumped out of that tree and grabbed his old .45-70 up but that snake was gone!

He said, "What do you want to do?"

I said, "I'm goin' home! I had enough of this today."

So we went back down Stagecoach Road, cut across the field, stopped at Uncle Will's house. He's layin' down but we went on in anyway. We never knock; we jist go on in. He was our friend and he let us do whatever we wanted to. We told 'im what we'd gotten into, how the snake had put us up there on that platform and how he'd layed there and looked up at us. All we had was an old hammer to throw at 'im. We was in trouble and then lightnin' struck that pine tree down there and sent Ole Joe, the gator, right through the sawgrass and sent the snake westward. But our guns was on the ground. So Byron got his quick, but the snake was gone.

"Listen, boys! Y'all need to stay away from that place. That's a bad, bad place."

We said, "Well Uncle Will, we got to do what we got to do. We got to catch that snake."

I come on home. 'Course you know what day this is, this is Saturday. Done got to take another bath. I ain't even dirty. I could wash my feet and go to bed and I'd be all right. But I know my mama ain't gonna hear of that. Too much bathin' in a week! But whenever she says, "You gonna do this," I don't argue with her 'cause I know I'm gonna lose. So I jist go ahead and do what she wants me to do.

Well, Sunday mornin' I put on my church clothes and went to church. I didn't sleep good that night. I dreamed of that snake. I dreamed that thang caught Byron and it caught me. I dreamed it climbed up that tree, and we beat it in the head with the hammer. It still crawled off. I had all kinds of dreams. My brother said, "You wiggled so much in that bed I couldn't sleep."

I said, "That ain't nothin'. I couldn't sleep either." So I told 'im what went on with that snake.

He said, "I'd think you'd know to stay away from that thang."

I said, "Well, I can't stay away. I done gone too far with it."

So we went to church Sunday mornin' and the preacher preached. He kind of preached towards me and Byron again. But we don't care. We jist gonna have to do what we gonna have to do.

Monday mornin' we went to school. It was the same ole stuff—A's and B's and C's and you got to study. You don't want to be a dummy whenever you get old. And we was in love with our teachers. They was the nicest people you ever wanted to meet.

We et in the lunchroom. Cost a nickel to eat there. My daddy couldn't afford the 25 cents, so he gave the school sweet taters and beans and peas and okra, and all the stuff he grew. He grew jist 'bout everythin'. Everythin' we et he either grew or killed it and then we et it.

The Swamp

Chapter 51

Well, Friday come. Byron said, "What do you want to do tomorrow?"

I said, "I don't want to go to that swamp!" I didn't want to go back to Lake Denham Swamp for a while. I'd had enough of that place for a bit.

He said, "Me neither. What do you want to do?"

"Why don't we go catch us a soft shell turtle and we'll take it down to Uncle Will? He don't feel so good."

I said, "That sounds good."

So Saturday mornin' 'bout 8 o'clock I go across the field. Byron was out there in the backyard eatin' mulberries. They was 'bout all gone. The birds et all of 'em. The bugs was in 'em purty bad whenever it was late in the season like this. But you don't worry 'bout the bugs; you jist go ahead and eat 'em, 'cause they won't hurt you. I tell 'im, "Let's go get the boat and go down to Bugg Spring Run and see if we can catch a soft shell turtle."

He said, "Alright."

So he go down and get the piece of wire we always use. He likes to oar the boat. So I got in front. We seen one ole gator turtle, but he'd be so strong that I doubt we could eat 'im. So we went on down to Bugg Spring Run and to Helena Run, and we still hadn't seen nothin'. We turned around and come back. We'd took our rifles out of the boat. So we put them back in the boat. We'd already had one encounter with the gator and the snake, and we almost got caught with the snake, so we ain't comin' down there no more without a rifle to shoot that thang if we have to.

We went a little further down and seen a turtle, but he was runnin' as fast as we could go. Come to find out, it works better at night. We can catch more soft shells at night with the piece of wire.

They's some men floats out there in Lake Denham where they swim up on the board. If they catch a turtle they hook the turtle there. And there's a man out there that shoots 'em in the head with a .22 and throws 'em in a boat and then cleans 'em. He could clean one in 'bout a second.

We went back down and pulled the boat back up. The boat hadn't leaked. We done a good job fixin' it. We still hadn't got even with ole Bill for shootin' a hole in the bottom of it. That's somethin' else we got to do.

We went back to the tree stand and got this little resin ball out and pulled on it. That thang could sing! Byron pulled on it and it made a weird sound. We stringed it a little bit and we beat it a little bit. That would keep all them people out of the Spring 'cause we didn't want 'em down in there. We went back by Uncle Will's house. He still warn't feelin' so good so we jist went on home. We figured next week we'd do somethin' different.

Another week went by and I said, "Let's go off there in the woods. Maybe we can see that snake and get 'im with our rifles." We went down, climbed on our platform, layed there and then we heared it. Bill!

We heared 'im; we saw 'im whenever he backed up into this place. He made us mad, 'cause we knowed he was gonna do somethin'. He got out and walked down into Cason Hammock. He had his shotgun with 'im. We heared 'im shoot. He'd shot another hole in that house we had up in that tree.

I said, "He might a have shot you!"

Byron said, "I could have shot a hole in his ear!"

I told 'im, "Well, we better off jist to leave 'im alone. But we ain't gonna put up with no more of his stuff." So we'd already taken and done everythin' to 'im we could think of. We layed up there for 2 or 3 more hours; nothin' happened. Then he got in his old car and drove off down the road.

Oops! The Game Warden

Chapter 52

We got to thinkin' and said, "You know what? We better go and check." And sure enough Bill had shot a hole in our skin on the log that we beat on. The one where we'd killed one hog before. So we fixed the hole up the best we could. Then Byron said that Uncle Will said, if we could take a hole and cut into the end of that thang, we could put a rosin ball on it. Then we could scare everythin' in them woods.

So we decided that's what we'd do that day. We ripped a hole in it, tied a knot in the other end, and went over there where there was turpentine in the pine trees. We got us a rosin ball off it. We already had one. If we pulled the string on it, it'd make a noise and then we beat on it.

Byron stretched that thang out and put the ball across it. I tell you, everythin' in them woods left. I mean they left! None of it stayed there. Even the frogs quit hollerin'. I ain't never heared such in all my life. It was fun. So then we put a resin ball on a string and it'd give a different sound. We'd beat on it and then we'd blow on our bamboo thangs like those people in Australia do. We had that whole woods a vibratin' down there. They warn't nobody want to come in that thang.

It was gettin' to be wintertime and gettin a little chilly. So we built up a little fire, cooked us a squirrel. We'd et all the squirrels up in them woods. Then we said, "Well, time to go home. It's fixin' to be a little bit late and it's gettin' darker earlier now." We cut across and went by Uncle

Will's. He still warn't feelin' good. He'd drunk all of that shine like he usually does.

So we decided we wouldn't wade in the marsh. We'd go straight on up the clay road. We got up the clay road and guess who was sittin' there? The game warden.

He said, "Boys, what y'all huntin?"

We said, "We huntin' that big old rattlesnake."

He said, "What kind of rattlesnake?"

Said, "It run 'bout 30 foot long. We tryin' to kill 'im. The snake man in Okella, he'll buy 'im from us if we kill 'im."

He said, "There ain't no rattlesnake 30 foot long." He said, "I been in the woods all my life."

We told 'im, "Well, you might never seen 'im, but we seen 'im. He put us up a tree."

He said, "Well, whenever you kill 'im, call me."

We said, "Ok."

He said, "You boys shootin' them squirrels over there?"

We said, "Not squirrels."

He said, "I see y'all runnin' around with all them squirrels. I hear all them noises over there. I never heared such a noise in all my life. I didn't know what was out there. That thang, I ain't never heared a sound like that before."

We told 'im, "We don't know what you're talkin' 'bout."

He said, "I think you boys do know what I'm talkin' 'bout." He said, "What y'all shootin' over there?"

We said, "We ain't shootin."

He said, "Rabbits? Alligators? Y'all shootin' them squirrels over there. Y'all shootin' them alligators over there."

We said, "We're not shootin' them alligators. We don't want to skin 'em. We don't skin alligators. We don't want to go to jail."

He said, "Then I'll tell you somethin' else, boys. Y'all plaited them bird traps over there and I found 'em. And I got 'em in the trunk of my car. I ain't gonna give 'em back to you. That's against the law to trap quail. Y'all over there trappin quail. Everybody knows who did it."

We jist didn't answer 'im. He said, "But I got the traps in the back of my car. I got them steel traps you had in there."

We said, "We ain't got no steel traps. Them thangs cost money and we ain't got no money."

"Oh. Ok. What kind of rifle is that you're shootin' there boy?"

Byron said, ".45-70."

"You shoot that purty good?"

"Yeah, I shoot that purty good."

He said, "You won that contest?"

He said, "Yes, sir, I did."

He said, "Ok, that's good. Well, you boys better be careful back there. Don't shoot any of them gators or the squirrels back there. They're not in season."

I said, "Yes, sir."

Well, he left and I went on down the road and went home. Supper was ready. We et and then here come my mama with a bottle and a spoon. I tried to alibi every way I could but she jist said, "You can take this stuff in the bottle, but you still need to take a bath."

I said, "I'll take a bath." I did and then went to bed and fell asleep. I don't even 'member my brother comin' in. I don't know if he stuck his cold feet on me or not.

Tomorrow's another day.

Friendship

Chapter 53

I got up, put my Sunday go-to-meetin' clothes on and went to church, and then back home. I changed clothes and we et lunch. Then I went out to play with the pigs. Them little pigs is a-growin'. I like to rub 'em. They was one of them especially liked it. He'd see me comin' and he would lay down so's I could rub 'is belly.

Then we had them guinea hens. You could hear them cacklin' out there. I had to go out there and get the guinea eggs. We didn't eat the guineas much. They's all dark meat, but we did eat them once in a while. And that old rooster guinea, if he'd get a chance he'd peck you. He'd do whatever he could to get even with you. He didn't want you messin' with them hens.

I used to watch them durin' a storm. If a hurricane would come, they'd be roostin' in an orange tree. They'd be there and the wind would be blowin' and they'd be rockin' back and forth. I couldn't understand how they could hold on to the limb like that. Then I found out, they squat down their legs.

So, I went to church Sunday night and walked by the depot. I didn't walk by that ole two-story house. I was still scared of it. Then I went home to bed. All week we had school; nothin' important there.

Saturday we got up, went over to Uncle Will's an' was listenin' to 'im tell all those ole tales up there that he did. We loved 'im. He was a fine ole man.

Then Byron said, "What do you want to do? We can go over to the creek and float down the creek."

I said, "Too cold. I don't want to go over there whenever it's cold like this."

He said, "Yeah, it is kinda cold. My mama told me I had to rake them yards."

I said, "Well, I'll go over and help you rake the yards."

So we raked the front yard and the back yard. They was all ole trees there.

Byron said, "You know, I got one of them old guns that Concord had. I want to shoot that thang and see what it does."

So we went out down by the hog pen. He thought, *I might as well let Larry shoot it. He never shot a rifle before.* So he handed it to 'im and told 'im to shoot that limb up there. He pulled the trigger and it hit. That bullet must-a been 40 years old. Whenever it left the gun, it was moving! It was a live bullet. It hit that limb up there and that limb jist leaned over. It didn't fall; it cut a big ole hole right through it. Larry said that it hurt 'im.

But Byron said, "Oh, you jist an ole sissy is all. You ain't hurt."

We went back to the house to put the rifle up. Then we went down to the hog pen to swing on the swings a little bit. I said, "We ought to go see 'bout Uncle Will." So we went down the clay road, 'cause the water done got so cold down there.

We went to his house. He was layin' on his bed. He still didn't feel good. So we asked 'im, "What do you need?" But he said he don't need nothin'. Said he'd be alright in a few days. So we left Uncle Will's house and come back down the road through the woods. We go down to the spring and there was a big ole gator waitin' out there on a log on the far side. Well, it jist warn't gettin' excitin' that day, so I went home.

I walked down by the store, took a right and went down by the depot. The man who runs the depot, he was down there workin' on Saturday. He don't usually work on Saturday, but I guess he had some-thin' he had to do down there. I walked on by and went to the hog pen. When I went down by the house and stayed in the dirt road. My mama said, "What are you doin' home so early?"

I said, "I guess there jist ain't nothin' to do today."

She said, "Ok. That's fine."

She had made some apple turnovers and baked sweet taters. I said, "Byron would like to have 'im a sweet tater."

She said, "Well, go on over there and take 'im some, and bring Byron back and I'll cut your hair and I'll cut his hair too."

She had a pair of them ole clippers she used. It cut one hair and pulled one. So I took 4-5 sweet taters over and told 'im my mama told me to come over and give 'im some sweet taters. She was cuttin' my hair and she'd cut his too.

So he come over and my mama cut our hair. Byron stayed 'bout an hour. I offered 'im another sweet tater and he's stay another hour, even when he knowed he was gonna get his behind tore up, he'd still stay. (I believe if I called 'im today and told 'im I had cooked some sweet taters he'd come right over.)

Then Sunday we went to church and Monday we went to school. School was cold that day so we built a fire in the woodstove. We needed to put wood in it. The auditorium and the bathroom didn't have no heat or runnin' water in 'em. So we went there across the field and the older boys carried water in.

The grass already turned brown. Thangs warn't goin' so good. We were all jist at the end of our rope, and you could tell that people was tired and had endured the war. Lots of people had died in it. But everybody knowed they must go on. Thangs was scarce.

We gathered up all the old aluminum and the rubber and everythin' else that was used in the war. The soldiers was all around Okahumpka. They'd sit there in the search lights at night. That's where they thought the Germans would be if they come in and attacked America. They sunk ships around Okahumpka.

Out with my Dad

Chapter 54

I was gettin' ready for bed; went to wash my feet and my face and my hands and then I'd go to bed. My dad informed me that I didn't have school the next day 'cause it was Teacher's Day, so he wanted me to go to the field with 'im.

I said, "Ok."

The next mornin' we got up at 6 and et breakfast. He cooked me 2 little fish and 2 little biskits with some jelly in it and put it in a little old tin like he always carried. We took off to the field. It was cool, not real cold, but I had a coat on. They cleared to start plantin' in January or February, or whenever they could to get an early crop of watermelons by July 4. I don't know if that was a big day that watermelon sold or not but I went to the field with 'im.

He said, "Now, we got git to work." So we got to the mule lot. We had a big stack of peanut hay there that we fed 'em. My dad said that the peanut hay makes the mules work better. He said, "Here's a .22 and a box of bullets. Go kill the possums, the coons, the rattle snakes, the fox squirrels and all them gophers." He said, "Kill every one of them gophers. What they do is, whenever they see a watermelon vine, they chew on it and eat it up."

I said, "Ok, I can do that."

He said, "But watch out for snakes."

I said, "Ok, I'll watch out for snakes."

So I left the truck and walked. They was a big prairie in there. It was all the way at the other side of the cemetery. They was in an orange grove, but he'd cut all the trees down. They said where you bulldoze the ground, you can't grow watermelons, but that ain't true. It was jist somethin' they jist don't like to do.

Well, I got over there and first thang I saw was 2 old sand hill cranes out there makin' dents. They sure was purty. Got a big old red head on 'em and they was makin' sounds. They sound like they tryin' to tear the woods up. I sat there and watched 'em tear up the ground.

Then I hear that sound. I knowed what it was. I'd heared it a million times. It was a buzz tail and he was a-singin'. So I eased by it. Got to lookin' and saw 'im. I shot 'im upside the head. I said to myself, "You know what? Bet you there's another one there." So I kept a watchin' and finally I saw it move. I shot it.

So then I went back to the truck and got me some rags there he had rolled up in a ball and you put high life on 'em. I don't know what high life is, but I know the gophers don't like it. And I throwed it down that gopher hole. Whenever you do that, them gophers is dead!

I went back to where I killed the rattlesnakes. I was cautious 'cause rattlesnakes run in bunches. I didn't see no more. I eased 'round the pond and saw an ole gator. You could see where that bullet had hit 'im across the head. Didn't even make 'im mad; his brain isn't big enough. All he wanted to do was get 'imself somethin' to eat, so I let 'im go by. At one time I'd have killed 'im and skinned 'im. But he was a little too far out there for me to go get his skin and I warn't 'bout to waste 'em.

I eased on around farther, got back purty nearly back to the truck, and then I heared it. I knowed what that sound was. I made me a turkey call. And I called and he answered. And I called again and he answered. I said, "He's comin' to me." I called and out walked an ole white turkey. I thought, *Whew Doggie! If there had been a red tail on that thang, I'd have shot it*. But my dad said, "Don't shoot that turkey. He belongs to that man up there on the hill."

We got back to the truck and my dad said, "It 'bout time to go home."

We got back in the truck and started down the road. Of course, one of the workers was sittin' up front with us and the rest of 'em was ridin' in the back. They was probably 5 or 6 of 'em. They used axes all day long and cross-cut saws. They'd bring in the big trees. Some of 'em would burn brush to kill 'em. Them axes was 9 pounds and they'd swing 'em all day long. They was macho men!

Whenever they cut them trees down out there they found they had a little worm they called the "fire worm". So they tightened their shirts up real tight and buttoned 'em up. I'm tellin' you, them fire worms burn you up. But they found that if they took and put vinegar on 'em it helped. But they still burned them up.

I said, "Stop, stop, stop!" I said, "Let me get one of them gators." The little ole gator was 'bout 6 inches long.

He said, "Ok." So I got it. I was sittin' in the front seat and I'd stick that gator on the knob. He'd bite it. Them gators will bite anythin'. I think they's born bitin'. I run my thumb by and he bit it. I screamed bloody murder. I got down on the floorboard, got a hammer and beat that thang in the head until it turned loose of my thumb.

My dad said, "You got to do somethin' with that, boy. We got to go ahead and get some turpentine on your thumb." So we went out there where they had some turpentine in the pine. Got some of that and wrapped it around my thumb with one of the rags. Ain't no tellin' where that rag had been, but that's alright. That bite set me on fire.

We got back to the truck and he said, "Why don't you catch another one of them thangs and let me see what's happenin'?" Now both men in the front seat was a-laughin'.

We got home and my mama had supper ready. She'd made some cat-eyed biskits and cooked up some of that pork that she'd put up. She said, "What's the matter with your thumb?"

I said, "That gator bit me."

She said, "Gator bit?"

Dad said, "Yeah, he caught 'im a little ole gator and he thought he could handle that but the gator et 'im up." He was laughin' 'bout it. I didn't find it a bit funny. I went in there and et and I was tired. I'd been all day long out there in them woods. He took and skinned them rattlesnakes. He said there was a man in town that would give me a dollar apiece for 'em and he'd probably give it to 'im. They used 'em for hat bands.

So I washed my face, washed my hands, washed my feet and I went to bed. I don't remember nothin' 'til the next mornin'. We layed up in that ole feather bed. You got to bed cold and in jist a few minutes you'd be jist as warm as toast.

Bill Botheration

Chapter 55

Mornin's a-comin'. Six o'clock and my daddy had breakfast ready. We went to school all week, and on Friday Byron said, "What we gonna do?"

I said, "Well, let's go over there to the swamp and see if there's anythin' there. Maybe we can see that snake. Maybe he's settled down a little bit."

He said, 'I ain't goin' in there without a gun."

I said, "I ain't either."

So the next mornin' as we left, Byron said, "You got any money?"

I said, "I got 2 cents."

He said, "I got 1 cent. Let's go see the man down at the grocery store that sells the big candy bars. We can take 1 over to Uncle Will for 'im since he ain't feelin' good."

I said, "Ok." So we went down to the grocery store and told the man at the store that we had 3 cents and wanted to get Uncle Will one of 'em Black Cow candy bars. He looked at us and said, "Boys, I'll tell you what I'll do. I'll give y'all two of 'em, and what I want is a nice fish."

We said, "We can do that. We can catch them fish. Can we do it next Friday? We'll clean 'im and we'll bring 'im to you ready to cook."

So we was goin' down the road and Byron said, 'You know what? Why don't we keep one of these candy bars and give the other 1 to

Uncle Will?"

Said, "That'd be fine with me."

He said, "We can eat it over there on that platform."

Said, "That's fine." So we stopped by Byron's house and got our rifles. We didn't wade across that pond over there; it's still too cold. We got over there to the woods and decided we'd go over there and get on the platform down by Lake Denham Swamp. We got a better chance of seein' that snake over there.

We made sure we looked in the woods to see if it hadn't crawled down through there or anythin'. And it hadn't. 'Bout 9 o'clock we heared somebody comin'. I said, "That sounds like ole Bill."

Sure enough, guess who pulled up? Ole Bill! He's back there in them trees where he hid his truck. He'd probably gone around and shot another hole in that thang. He didn't come over to where we was at 'cause he had to wade that mud. Our feet was cold where we waded in. We tried wrappin' them up and stuff but there warn't no way to keep 'em warm. So we'd go in there barefooted and then we'd put our socks and shoes back on when we got out. We would dry our feet with some moss.

Said, "Listen. He's goin' around where our stand is at."

Byron said, "I bet he is." So we got down off that platform and waded back across there. There was his old cut-off car.

We said, "Hmm. You know what, we ain't never got even with 'im for that last round he did to us. Well, this time, we get even with 'im."

We had picked up an ole 3H cable off the side of the road and took it down there into the woods. He backed up real close to an ole water oak. We wrapped that cable around that ole wooden body on that truck. We tied that cable to that tree and we put a double hitch in it so it would hold. Cable is hard to tie. We eased back up away and we layed up there and we ate our Black Cow candy bar. We got all through with that candy and we was thinkin' 'bout what-all we could do.

We decided we could get back down, but then we saw 'im. He was comin' out. So we hid up in the trees. Then I said, "You know what? If we run out there in front of 'im, he'll try to run us down with that ole truck."

Byron said, "Let's do it."

So he started out and we ran out in front of 'im. He put it in low gear and floored it. It snatched that truck body right off! He had his gun in his hand. The truck throwed 'im off into the dirt, skinned 'im all up and he stuck the end of that gun barrel in the dirt. He saw us and I guess he was gonna shoot us.

But when he got up and pulled the trigger that thang was full of dirt and it corked up the barrel of that shotgun. It knocked 'im flat on the ground. We run in circles back through the trees, 'cause if he caught us out in the open he would take a whippin' on us like you wouldn't believe.

We come back round where the ole truck was at and we saw 'im goin' down ole Stagecoach Road. I guess he was jist gonna walk home. He looked kind of a bad sight. We took the cable off that truck body 'cause we didn't want anybody to know what happened. We took the cable and then waded back 'cross Lake Denham Swamp. We was laughin' so much it jist hurt. It was funny. We done got even with 'im. He'll probably shoot us both.

Anyways, we went back and said, "Let's go to Uncle Will's." He was sittin' out by the fire and he said he still felt bad. We wanted to know if there was anythin' we could do for 'im. He jist said that he appreciated the candy bar and that he'd eat it someday. We was already wet so we waded across that little ole marsh and went back behind Byron's house.

Byron's little brother was down there swingin' on the swing. He still had green arms and a red face. We had a red face too. I don't know when that stuff's gonna come off. So we was still Injuns. Larry's headdress looked purty good once he got them buzzard feathers out of it.

I told Byron, "I'm gonna go home." I went on home. It was Saturday; you know what that means. Another of 'em baths. So I took my bath, et supper and my mama asked me what we was doin' over in that swamp. I jist said, "Oh, nothin'."

She said, "Well, before you go to bed, I need you to walk down to the store and get me a loaf of bread."

I said, "Ok."

She gave me 9 cents and said, "You can have the other penny."

I said, "Ok." So I got me a penny Black Cow candy bar. I would save the other half for Byron. We done et that other one. But guess what? There was ole Bill. He didn't look good. His face was skinned; his arms was skinned. He said, "You boys sure messed me up."

I said, "Messed you up how?"

Said, "Y'all pulled the body off my truck."

I said, "Well, I don't know how me and Byron could pull the body off your truck."

He said, "Well, somebody did."

I said, "Maybe that man saw you run across his yard the other night and is mad at you."

He said, "How do you know 'bout that?"

"Well, everybody knows he saw you."

He said, "Well, I better stay away from down there then."

"Yeah, if I was you I'd stay away."

So the night ended. I went home. I was scared. I knowed he might be down there by the post office or the depot and he'd settle up with me. But he didn't. I think he had 'bout enough of us. I put the bread in the bread safe. The safe is the screened in thang you use to put the food in to keep the flies out and such. I went in and went to bed. My brother come in early that night. I guess he worked hard all day. He had a new job at the grocery store.

The Grapefruit Cure

Chapter 56

The next mornin' was Sunday. Got up put on my Sunday go-to-meetin' clothes and went to church. The preacher preached 'bout gettin' along with others. Guess he was preachin' at me and Byron again.

Then I come home. I didn't feel too good. Maybe I was gettin' a cold or somethin'. So I told my mama, I said, "I think I'm gettin' a cold."

She said, "Probably from wadin' in that cold water. I got somethin' for you to take for it."

So she went outside and got one of 'em grapefruit. She peeled it, took that white part in there and cooked it in the fryin' pan 'til it turned into a black-lookin' syrup. Then she rolled it up. Boy, that thang tastes bad. But I knowed that I could either do the easy way or the hard way.

She said, "Put it on your tongue, but don't swallow it." Boy, was it bitter!!!

Every little bit she'd say, "Let me see it." It had melted down. When it melted down she said, "Ok, you can go to bed now. You will break out in a sweat but when you do, don't get out from underneath the covers or you'll get pneumonia." It was called catula. It would jist make you sleepy and sweaty.

The next mornin' I got up and I felt purty good but coulda felt better. I went to school anyway. The teacher was talkin' 'bout school was gonna let out real soon and everybody'd be able to do what they wanted to do in the summertime. So I was lookin' forward to that.

The Swamp

Chapter 57

The weekend ended, and by Friday we got out of school for the summer. We grabbed our rods and we went down to Shaw Pond. We waded out to 'bout waist-deep, had us a piece of wire tied to our britches. You wore long britches there and you wore an ole pair of shoes if you had 'em, 'cause that ole grass in there, it'd cut red streaks all over you. You even wore a long sleeve shirt when you waded down in there.

There was plenty of bass. We caught 15-20. We took one by Uncle Will's and we cleaned it too. Then we cleaned the rest of 'em and flayed them. We didn't take the skin off 'cause people like the skin. That's what makes 'em good.

We went down to the man at the grocery store and took 'em down in a flour sack. We said, "Here's your fish."

He looked at 'em and said, "Oh boy, them look good."

I said, "They's good. We caught 'em out there at Shaw Pond. That's a clean pond."

He said, "They let you fish there?"

We said, "They do if we don't get caught."

He said, "Y'all been caught in there?"

We said, "No. If that man come by we run in them meadows and he can't find us in there."

Said, "Oh, Ok. Well, I appreciate the fish. I'm gonna give y'all a Coke, too." So he gave us one of them six-ounce Cokes. My, My, whew, that thang was good. We drank it down 'cause durin' the war, they didn't put Cokes out for sale. They was a nickel apiece, but you couldn't jist take and get 'em anywhere. Whenever he'd get 'em he'd save 'em out there in the back and sell 'em to the people that done business with 'im. We drunk them drinks and put them bottles back in the box there 'cause the bottles was a nickel apiece.

We went back down the road there and I told Byron, I said, "Well, I'm goin' home. I'll see you tomorrow."

He said, "What do you want to do tomorrow?"

I said, "Oh, I don't know." Said, "You wanna go over to the creek and see if we can shoot a bass?"

He said, "Ok."

So we eased over to the creek along the ridge the next mornin', but we didn't see no bass. We saw one ole moccasin, and we killed it. He decided he'd waste a shell on one of 'em thangs and said, "Every time I see 'em around, I got to kill 'em." It was a big ole moccasin too, 'bout 3 feet long and as big as your leg. So we walked all along the edge. We didn't bring anythin' for lunch, so we cut one of them cabbage palms down and cut the top out of it. That stuff ain't no good if it ain't cooked. But we et some of it anyway. The way you tell if it's too tough is, if it won't break, it's too tough. So we et some of that. Got us some water too; that always helps.

It was gettin' to be 'bout 4 o'clock and I said, "Let's go home." So we walked down by Sally's Pond. We walked on there across the ditch toward 48 and went in the back way by the dairy.

I said, "Well, I'm goin' home. Listen, I hear that thang over yonder in that ole post office? Listen."

Boom, boom, boom, boom, boom, boom, boom.

I said, "That thang, the booger's in there now. Hear it?"

We went across the railroad tracks and went down there where the depot was. We couldn't get a good view of that, so we went back down where the outhouses was at behind the house. He said, "There you go; it's by the window." He up and raised up and shot where he figured that ole booger would have been. Guess what happened?

The booger turned 'im loose. That fella run down them back stairs. He was hittin' 'bout every tenth step. He come to the bottom and jumped that fence. Byron said, "You know, he's scared!"

We didn't know who he was. We didn't care, but we saved 'im from the booger. We went back in there and looked. You could see where the ball was at the end. And we looked on the other side where he had tore that board up. I said, "Do you think that booger's layin' in there?"

He said, "Probably is."

I said, "But I ain't goin' up there to find out. I ain't that brave." So we went on home. I warn't afraid of that place no more. That booger was dead! He's dead!

I got up the next mornin, and went to church. 'Course I had to have that bath before I went to bed. *Well,* I thought, *My, my, gettin' warmer all the time.*

I walked right by that old post office; ain't nothin' in there that would scare me no more. That booger's gone! I walked down and went to church and come home. We et lunch and I went out back to scratch the belly on them ole pigs. They sure was fun. They rollin' too. And you could take a curry comb and put it on a stick and reach in there. They'd "oink, oink, oink."

All week I went to school. Come Friday and Byron said, "We goin' over to the swamp?"

I tell 'im, "Yeah." So I come over to Byron's house. We waded across the pond. The water had warmed up a little bit. They was turtles all over that log so we caught us 2 or 3 of 'em and throwed 'em back in. They warn't nothin' in there. It warn't very deep, 'bout waist deep.

We went to Uncle Will's and he was sittin' outside by the fire. He sure didn't feel good; you could tell he was sick. I said, "Uncle Will, what seems to be the problem?"

He said, "I don't know, boys, but I'll tell you what. I sure don't feel good."

We said, "Well, we'll be back here in a little while. We're goin' to go down there and see if we can see that snake."

He said, "Ok, but be careful. I don't want you to go down there."

We said, "We got to. We got to catch that snake and get us a hundred dollars."

He said, "Boys, if somethin' happened to you down there, my goodness, I'd never get over it." We got caught one time without our guns, but we ain't gettin' caught again.

We went down and saw that Bill had tied the body on his truck. I bet he had it on better this time than he had last time. We looked and you could see where that cable was around that tree. We had that cable hidden down in them woods. So we ease on down and said, "Let's go down and see what we can see."

We climbed up on our platform. The wind was blowin' a little bit and it was a little chilly, but not bad. I figured we was a little bit cold. We took our shoes off and put on a pair of socks. Mine had turned black. My mama would skin my hide!

We layed up there for a couple of hours. Ole Joe, the gator, he come swimmin' down the canal. We watched 'im. He knowed we was up that tree and he knowed he was gonna bother us. We layed there a little while. Then Byron touched me and gave me the signal to be quiet. I layed there and I listened. He said, "He's comin'!" He pushed the safety off on his gun and said, 'Hear it?"

"Yeah."

He said, "Them bushes is shaking! Them bushes is shaking!"

I said, "Yeah, they are!"

"When he sticks his head out, I'm gonna kill 'im." But out stepped that ole boar hog! We ain't seen 'im in a while. He was a gruntin' and a snortin' around there. I said, "He almost made me have a heart attack. My heart was a-beatin'!"

Byron said, "I almost shot 'im."

I said, "Yeah, but he ain't hurtin' nothin'."

He went on a little ways and the next thang we knowed that old sow come by with eight of them little pigs. They was big enough to eat, but we was snake huntin' so we let the pigs go on by. They was right by the tree stand; they didn't see us, or hear us, or smell us, or nothin'. They swam out and then waded through the mud and then went northwest. And then it was quiet.

We looked at the pine tree over there and we saw where lightnin' struck it. It died. All the leaves, the needles were really fallin' off it. We said, "We sure hate that thang had to die." It was a big ole pine but it had saved our lives. It sure did.

It got to be 'bout 4 o'clock. We eased by there under the tree, waded across and walked down through the grove to see if the snake had been there. It hadn't been. We went back by Uncle Will's. He jist warn't lookin' good. He was sittin' out there by the fire. I told 'im, "Uncle Will, have you had anythin' to eat?"

He said, "Yeah, my sister brought me somethin' to eat."

I said, "Ok."

He said, "She does 'bout everythin'. She come down here and brought me some cornbread and some beans and a big piece of ham. I ain't finished that pig either. You want some of it?"

We said, "No, but if you need us, you let us know. We'll take care of it."

Game Warden Troubles

Chapter 58

We decided we wouldn't wade across the marsh; we'd go up through the clay road. So we went up to the clay road and there he sat again. The game warden. He said, "Boys, what y'all kill today?"

We said, "The only thang we killed was time."

He said, "I heared you had some excitement over there in the woods."

We said, "When was that?"

He said, "Some fella stuck a rifle in the dirt and then pulled the trigger."

We said, "Oh yeah, that was Bill. He does stuff like that."

He said, "He said y'all did it."

I said, "We didn't do it."

"You didn't do it?"

I said, "No we didn't do it. How would we put dirt down his gun barrel with 'im carryin' the gun?"

He said, "Y'all tied the cable on the back of his truck?"

Byron said, "You think we'd do somethin' like that?"

He said, "Yeah, I do. What'd he do to you?"

I said, "Oh, he didn't do nothin' to us. We don't have no trouble with 'im."

The warden said, "All right. But now there ain't no bird traps over there, is there?"

"No, there ain't no bird traps."

He said, "Alright."

Byron said, "We's goin' home."

So the warden left and I turned to Byron and said, "You know what? We need to catch us some quail in them bird traps."

He said, "Yeah, I agree with you."

Sunday we went to Sunday School and church. The preacher preached 'bout all them people who do all them thangs they ain't supposed to be doin' anyway.

"Yes, sir, we got that!"

We went over there and cut us some palm fronds. We plaited them thangs up and made us some more traps. The secret to the thang is to make it so you barely touch it. We didn't want to catch no rattlesnakes. My dad come home and said, "What are you makin'?"

I said, "Quail traps."

He said, "Yeah, I've made a million like that. How many quail y'all caught?"

We said, "A bunch of them."

He said, "That game warden, that's all he's after. So you watch 'im."

'Bout Thursday me and Byron went over there and put that scratch feed in the trap. We seen 'bout 5 traps, 'cause that's how many we made. Friday we'd go check on 'em.

What you do is, you take a piece of wire and you run it through that thang. You put it over that quail's head and shake it and pop his head. I knowed I was goin' to have to go across that field and that ole game warden would be there. I had 5 quail in my fingers and they was still alive. I didn't want to take the chance of killin' 'em and 'im walkin' up on me.

I was easin' on up through there, and I thought I saw his vehicle there, so I was gonna go a little bit east and go through the grove and miss 'im. But he still wound up in front of me with them five quail. I throwed my hands up and turned them thangs loose and they flew. He told me, he said, "Boy, I done caught you and I'm gonna take you to jail."

I said, "For what?"

He said, "For trappin' quail."

I said, "I ain't got no quail."

He said, "What? I saw you with them quail in your hand."

I said, "Yeah, I know you did. But them was pet quail."

He said, "They's no such thang." He said, "Look here, boy." He searched me; he looked in my pockets and he said, "I'm tellin' you what. One of these days I'm gonna catch both you boys and I'm gonna put you both in jail. You ain't been nothin' but a thorn in my side."

I told 'im, "Well, we ain't guilty."

He said, "Where's your traps at?"

I said, "I ain't got no traps."

He said, "I'll find 'em."

Well, if he can find 'em he can have 'em. I walked down across the field and walked right by that ole post office. I warn't afraid of that thang no more. That booger is gone! We found out later that fella who was up there was scared to death when that rifle fired. It was 'bout a foot from his head and that booger turned 'im loose. He said that he didn't go up there again 'cause he didn't know who shot at 'im.

So I went home, washed my feet and my face and my hands and et my supper before I went to bed. Boy, my feet was nasty! They had that ole mud and those shoes and socks. I washed them socks out the best I could. I told my mama I had to wash them. She said, "Yeah, you been wadin' in the mud again."

I said, "Yup."

She said, "I'll boil your shoes with 'em. Boil 'em in the wash pot." That'd clean 'bout everythin'.

Helpin' Out at the Springs

Chapter 59

Got up the next mornin'. It was Friday so I went to school. The teacher said, "Next week y'all are out of school for the week!" Whew Doggie!! She said, "There's a man here that wants to talk to y'all. He's from down at the Springs."

He said, "Boys, next week y'all are out of school. I want y'all to come down to the Springs and help me clean up. I'll give y'all a pair of shoes."

We told 'im, "Ok. We'll be ready."

They was 'bout 5 of us. The springs down there was lots of fun to go down to. We go down and pick up all the ole leaves and limbs and logs, and then in the afternoon we got to swim in the Springs. He was a nice man. For breakfast we got 2 eggs with grits and biskits and a Coke. For lunch we got a hot dog, 2 if you wanted, and a Coke. You got a hamburger with tomato on it and onion. I didn't like tomatoes, so I'd always get it and throw it in the bushes, so it looked like I et it.

And then we'd go down to the Springs and take our bath and go to bed. He did all the nice thangs for us and we really appreciated it. We went to the Springs that whole week. On Friday, he gave us all a pair of tennis shoes. And this time he gave us a quarter. I didn't know he was goin' to give us the quarter. I was pleased to get it.

Every one of us left and he said, "Well, we'll see you next year." We went back to the school to get the girls and they cleaned the house. I'll never forget 'im. He was jist really good to us. He said, "Boys, what are y'all gonna do this summer?"

And I said, "Byron and I gonna catch that snake."

He said, "Well, you better watch it, 'cause from what I hear he's a bad, bad snake."

The Swamp

Chapter 60

"Yes, he is." So we went on.

Saturday was comin' up. We found us an ole piano and Uncle Will told us if we'd take and get the fine wire out of that piano he'd tie it so we could catch that snake.

We said, "Ok."

We went down there and took a hammer and tore up that thang. That piano wire was hard to get out of it but we got it out. We got 'bout 8 or 9 pieces 'cause we didn't know which size Uncle Will would want. Then he took and scrawled out in the dirt what kind of thang we needed to build to catch the snake.

I said, "Ok. We got that."

We got some ole pipe layin' there and we got a big hammer. He said, "I want you to drive this thang in the ground, so once you catch 'im, he can't take and run off."

We told 'im, "Ok."

He showed us how to build a pen. We put chicken wire around it and Uncle Will said, "He'll jist crawl through that chicken wire; it's big enough."

So we got out some hardware cloth we'd found in the trash down there by the Springs. We took that hardware cloth and put it all around the backside. Then we put some more chicken wire on. On the front part we had a piece of glass. My mama said I could have one of 'em ole hens that warn't layin' no more. Told her I needed it to lay a trap with. She knowed what I was gonna do with it.

So Saturday mornin', we was ready. We gonna take and catch that snake. We made our snares up and put 'em on the front. We put that ole chicken in that thang and we set a snare up. We put the front so that the snake would have to reach his head through the wire to get it. Then he had 'bout 5 foot of wire he could play with. We set the trap and it warn't thirty seconds 'til we heared that flam-bammin' over there. So we run over there with our rifles! It was a possum!!

We knocked it in the head with a stick and layed it out on top of the pen. Then we went back in where ole Bill had parked his truck. He was waitin'.

Then we heared this commotion. I mean, it was a goin' on. You could hear it singin'. I said, "We got 'im! We got that snake!" So we run across the log and climbed up on our platform and sure 'nough, we had snared that rattlesnake!!!!

It saw us and it tried to run. Ole Joe, the gator, had to get involved in it too. He was over there on the right-hand side. He was gonna get 'im a meal out of it too. But we didn't want 'im to eat up our snake. So I said, "We'll have to kill ole Joe!"

Byron said, "If we don't he's gonna get our snake."

And he went, "POW!"

That snake done rared up 'bout three feet in the air. He was throwin' his head back and forth; I'm mean he was a goin'. Whew Doggie! I would have hated to been caught by that thang! He was goin' back and forth. He made a lunge and when he made a lunge it cut his head off! His head flew over to the side and the venom run out. I was scared! He was still strikin' at everythin' that was around. But we got 'im!!!

I told Byron, I said, "I'm goin' to go get a bucket to put the head in." We had a bucket with a hole in the side of it, but it would hold his head. Whenever I come back the snake had bled down and he quit movin', but the muscles on 'im was still workin'.

So Byron said, "I'm goin' home to get my daddy to come over with the truck. We'll load 'im up."

I said, "Ok. I'll be here."

We had the bucket loaded but I was still afraid to pick that snake up.

They was that ole yellow venom all over everythin'. Byron come back with his dad and they waded in on that island over there. His daddy had brought 2 other fellas with 'im to see the snake.

While they was gone I went ahead and skinned Ole Joe. I couldn't turn 'im over, so Byron helped me. We finished skinnin' 'im. Then we loaded the snake up on it and the gator too. That thang was heavy.

I picked up the bucket with the snake head and put it on the back of the truck. We took it all down to the store. We left the rifles at Byron's house 'cause we didn't need 'em at the store. We warn't gonna shoot ole Bill anyway.

Then we found out that Bill was in jail! Him and a fella got in a fight at the bar. So they put 'em in jail. So he warn't around.

They measured the snake at the store. With the head on it, it would have been 30 foot. Whew Doggie! What a snake! So we got Miss Sally to call the snake man in Okella. He said it'd take 'im 'bout an hour to get there.

So in 'bout an hour he showed up and the paper from Leesburg come down there to take pictures. I had never been on a camera before. I thought that was somethin' good. They took pictures of me and Byron with the snake and they layed the snake head out. It was a bad-lookin' thang! Wow! We done it!

The snake man come up but before he got there a fella come up and said, "You want to sell that-there hide?"

I said, "Well, we done promised it to the snake man in Okella."

He said, "I'll give you 200 dollars for it."

But I told 'im, "Well, we gave 'im our word and we gonna keep our word."

He said, "Ok."

The snake man walked up and looked and said, "Boys! I never believed it! I didn't believe that snake would be thirty-foot long. I ain't never seen a snake that big before in my life. I'd have took a thousand dollars for it alive."

I said, "Well, whenever you saw that thang down there when he was alive, you probably wouldn't have."

So we told 'im that the man had offered 200 dollars for it, he said, "Ok, I'll pay you that much for it."

I said, "We can skin it for you if you want us to."

He said, "Oh, no, I don't want to skin it. I want to have it like it is. I want to take 'im up and have 'im mounted."

We said, "Ok."

We took 'im up to the store and he come out and give Byron a 100 dollars in 1 dollar bills and he gave me 100 dollars in 1 dollar bills. We was rich!! We was rich!! Whew Doggie! We was rich!

So we decided we had to go tell Uncle Will that we'd killed the snake.

We went by his house and went in. "Uncle Will?" He was layin' on his ole bed. "We killed that rattlesnake! And we got paid for it. And we want to give you some of the money."

He said, "No, boys, I don't want none of your money. Y'all earned it. I'm glad you killed it and I'm glad it's over with."

We told 'im, "We are too."

Uncle Will said, "Boys, I don't feel good. I won't keep you no longer."

We said, "Alright."

He said, "I'm glad you killed it. I'm glad you killed it. You deserve the money."

We said, "Ok."

We left then and said, "Let's go down there and lay on the platform."

I said, "I ain't goin' without my gun."

So we went down where the old hen was still in the thang. I told 'im, I said, "I'm gonna take the hen back home so we can kill it."

We pulled the piece of glass up and that hen run out of that thang across the woods. I never seen it again. I don't know where it went. I would guess it was 'bout scared nearly to death for bein' in that thang. I knowed if I had been in that cage...

Tomorrow's another day.

A Really Big Adventure Ends

Chapter 61

My dad come home and said, "Well, how'd you do?"

I said, "We killed that big snake! We sold it and we got a hundred dollars apiece I got a 100 dollars in my pocket in 1 dollar bills. I'm rich."

He said, "Well, you need to take it out of your pocket. There ain't no sense in carrying that around. You'll get knocked in the head for it. But I'm glad you killed that snake."

I said, "But I'm sad 'bout it."

He said, "Yeah, I know. I've killed many, many deer. And sometimes I don't know why I killed 'em. But you do it. You jist did it and you did a good job with it and everybody knows that."

Saturday it was jist another day. We had fun, but I was kinda sad. I was sad 'cause what we were after, once we killed it, I didn't like what we had done. It was a living thang and we had took it away from the swamp. We had fought many a day to kill that thang. We had heartbreaks; we got scared. That thang nearly caught us.

That week I worked a little bit out there pickin' up taters. Byron worked with his dad who was in the poultry business. Then come Friday, I saw Byron and he said, "What we gonna do tomorrow?"

I said, 'Let's go down there and lay up in our house. We don't got to worry 'bout Bill 'cause he's in jail; there's nothin' to worry 'bout now that we got that snake hunt done."

He said, "You got it."

So, come Saturday mornin', I went across the field, took my .22. I warn't goin' down there without it. Got down and said, "Boy, ain't this somethin'? There ain't no snake here." We layed up there.

We'd killed the snake. Now, what were we gonna do? I'm almost sad over the fact that we killed that snake. The thang was, I was jist sad 'bout it. I knowed that it was a dangerous thang; I knowed that we had to do somethin' with it and I wanted a hundred dollars. But it's sad. I hope whenever they mount it, we get to go see it one day.

A Best Friend Passes On

Chapter 62

I went outside. Not much to do anyway. I went back there where the pigs is at. Got my curry comb out and scratched the belly on that one. He went "oink, oink, oink." He liked that. He'd seen me comin' and he'd run up there to the edge of fence.

My dad come runnin' and said, "Red, I got some bad news."

I said, "What's that?"

He said, "Will's dead."

I said, "What?"

He said, "Will's dead and they want you to come over there. I'll take you in the truck."

I said, "No, I'll go over there across the field." I went over there and I went by Byron's house. Byron was fixin' to leave.

He said, "Did they tell you that Will's dead?"

"Yes."

So we went over there to where he was at, but they already hauled 'im off. We cried. His sister was there and she held both of us. She said, "Boys, he loved you. He loved you young 'uns and he was scared to death y'all was gonna get hurt in that swamp."

We said, "We knowed he was in that swamp with us all the time."

She said, "Yeah, he was."

I said, "We was gonna split the money from killin' that snake with 'im."

She said, "Well, he don't need no money where he's goin'. He's in
a better place. But he loved you two boys. Now he left y'all everythin'
he owned. He left y'all 4 dollars. So you can split the4 dollars. Red, he
left you his rifle and Byron he left you his pistol. He left the pot that
he cooked in and the spoon and the fork. And he left you the corncob
pipe. He said he knowed y'all enjoyed that thang so much, so he left it
to you."

We said, "We didn't want 'im to die."

She said, "Well in life, that's what people do. He was an ole man.
He had lots of fun with you. He said for Byron to take the goats; he
knowed that's where them goats come from. He knowed all the time
whose goats they was. And Red, them chickens, you could have 'em for
your mama.

"He said your mama knowed all 'bout the thangs you tried to pull
on 'im and that he already knowed 'bout it. And he knowed 'bout the
game warden tryin' to catch y'all, so he'd go down there and run inter-
ference for you."

We said, "We didn't know that."

She said, "He was glad ole Bill went to jail. He was scared Bill was
gonna do somethin' to y'all. But he found out later on that Bill had
more troubles with y'all than he knowed what to do with. They gonna
bury Will Friday. I'll pick you up and take you to the funeral. "

We said, "Ok."

She went on to say, "He ate that Black Cow candy bar y'all gave 'im."

I said, "I'm glad he did. We should have give 'im both of 'em."

They put 'im in the hearse and we went to the funeral. It was up
there in Leesburg. We was goin' to set on the back row but she said,
"Oh, no."

We went out there and looked in the casket. I cried and cried. He
had on that ole straw hat that we give 'im and that red bandana we
bought 'im. They was all thangs that we'd give 'im. We was proud of
'im, and I think he was proud of us. I'm really gonna miss 'im.

So we sat in the front row of the church. I cried through the whole thang.
It was jist hard, so very hard. His sister sat between us and she held both of
us. We jist couldn't understand why he had to die. But he did.

We got in the car with the family. It warn't a big family, jist his sister and 2 of her kids. They was old now though. We went out to Yalaha; they had to go by Okahumpka to get to Yalaha and they had the funeral procession goin'. The grave was out there and was already dug. They had a piece of what looked like oil cloth over the grave so you could see it. We jist couldn't understand. They took and lowered 'im into the grave and the preacher said some words.

'Bout 2 or 3 weeks later, we went out there to his grave. We walked down to Yalaha, out there off the road. We saw where they buried 'im and they had a grave marker there, warn't as big as your hand. It said, "Will James." But it didn't give the day he was born, 'cause he didn't even know when he was born.

We went back and I got my .22 and Byron had his .45-70. We went down and climbed up on the tree. The varmints had cleaned up all the blood and stuff that was around there. I don't know if they ate that rattlesnake poison or not. They may have or not. Ole Joe, he done feed the catfish. We still had his hide. We was tryin' to figure out what to do with it. But we'd get somebody to take it, cure it and sell 'im for us. We didn't know how much he would bring. There warn't no buttons or warts on it. There warn't no cut places in it, so it was a really good hide. We done salted it down 'cause we knowed that the salt would draw out the moisture from the skin.

We climbed up on the platform and layed there a few minutes but said, "This ain't no fun; let's go over to the other one."

So we went to the other tree house and got out our corncob pipes. We got our mattresses out; we'd put 'em up underneath there. They still had a little ole hole in there where Bill shot it. We done put too much used tin over that one spot.

It's no fun now that Uncle Will is gone and it's jist different now since the snake's gone. We always had the anticipation of seein' 'em.

Well, we was jist layin' there smokin' our corncob pipes and we saw the bushes shakin'. Byron said, "I know what that is."

I said, "What is it?"

He said, "It's that ole boar hog. We done nicked his ears all up. Think I'll jist shoot his tail off."

I said, "No, let 'im have it. He got to have somethin' to twitch goin' through the woods."

But guess what? It walked out, but it warn't that ole boar hog. It was the sow and her pigs. Them pigs was 'bout 60-70 pounds, so they'd be good eatin'. But I didn't feel up to cleanin' one and he didn't either.

But he said, "I'd kill that one on the right." He pointed to the little sow. I said, "Ok." But he didn't.

We layed up there probably for an hour or so. Tomorrow's Saturday. Nope, I'm wrong; it ain't Saturday, it's Friday. We ain't got to go to school so that's why I got my days mixed up.

A Tombstone for Uncle Will

Chapter 63

Byron said, "Do you like that tombstone that Uncle Will's got over there?"

I said, "No, I don't." I said, "Why don't we take and buy 'im a tombstone? We got 204 dollars. So I'll go home and get my money. You meet me at the train station, and we'll catch the 11 o'clock train tomorrow. We'll go to Leesburg."

He said, "That's fine. We'll go up there and we'll buy 'im a 204 dollar tombstone, if they make one."

I said, "I don't know if we can buy one. I don't know what one costs." So we caught the 11 o'clock freight the next day. We was barefooted. We had on ragged shirts. Our faces was clean but our feet was dirty. We didn't have no shoes on. We got off at the depot in Leesburg and walked down the street there by the white man buryin' land and walked by the hospital. Then we went on through town.

We got on down to the black man buryin' land and we went to this place. We asked 'im if we could buy a tombstone and the man said, "Well, yeah, I can sell one. What do you want on it?"

We said, "We want 'Will James' and the date he died. And our names. Put 'We love you Will' and then put our names on it."

He said, "That'll be 320 dollars."

We said, "We only got 204 dollars."

He said, "Then I can't do it."

We said, "Well, can you make it a little bit smaller?"

He said, "I can't. The problem is cuttin' the names in."

"Oh."

He said, "Can't do it, boys."

We said, "Ok." So we left and were downhearted as we could be. We had that 204 dollars. We hoped they would sell us one, but they wouldn't. So we come on down and we walked by the tire repair shop.

Byron said, "There's a funeral home up there where they bury white people. Maybe he'll sell us a tombstone." So we walked in the door. We'd never been in one of them places before. It was quiet in there. Really quiet. It was even cool. So the fella at the front said, "May I help you boys?"

We said, "We want to buy a tombstone for our friend. Well, he's a black man, but he ain't got no tombstone on his grave and we want to buy 'im one."

He said, "Hmmm. Have you got the money?"

We said, "Yeah, we got the money; we got 204 dollars."

He said, "I'll tell you what. I'm fixin' to go somewhere. Why don't you come with me."

I said, "Oh, Ok."

He said, "We may be able to get you a tombstone." We went out there and got in that fancy car.

I told Byron, I said, "You think we ought to wash our feet before we get in here?"

But the man said, "No, no. Don't worry 'bout it. Y'all jist get in the back seat." So we got in the back seat and we drove down Ninth Street, got down Dixie Avenue and we stopped. We knowed where we was at. He said, "Boys, come on."

He parked up there and we walked through the door. There was all them people sittin' in there with coats and ties on.

I told Byron, I said, "We in the wrong place, but maybe we can get us a tombstone from here."

He said, "Ok, if we can get a tombstone that's fine."

The man that was in charge up there, his name was John. He said, "What's the boys with you?"

Said, "I'll tell you what we need."

John said, "Ok." So they put us down at the table, up front. I wanted to be back there the back, but they put us up front. I thought they were funnin' us for a little bit, but I don't guess they were.

Finally he said, "You boys, tell them what you want."

I said, "We got an ole colored friend of ours and he died. He got buried out in Yalaha and we want to buy a tombstone. We got 204 dollars; we killed that big snake and it's the money from that."

"Oh, y'all the ones that killed it?"

"Yeah. And he helped us kill it. We want to buy 'im a tombstone 'cause he don't have one."

So John got up and said, "Well, would y'all like to donate the money to the tombstone?"

The man in the back stood and said, "Hey look, I know a place that makes tombstones. I'll give these boys a tombstone if they tell me what they gonna put on it."

He said, "Ok."

Well, then they brought out dinner. I never seen 2 forks at one time. That meant somebody had to wash 'em twice. They brought that meat out that had some gravy at the top of it. Then some mashed taters, some green beans, a big ole glass of sweet tea and a slice of chocolate pie. Whew Doggie. We gobbled that stuff up like we had never et nothin' before. We et that piece of chocolate pie and guess what they did? They brought us another piece. And we et it too!

After we et pie we got up and they had their meetin'. One of 'em got up; it was the man that had the mercantile store. We didn't know what a mercantile store was but we knowed what a fish market was, and we knowed what a grocery store was, but we'd never heared of a mercantile store. He said, "Would you get them boys a pair of shoes?"

They said, "Oh yeah, we'll get them boys a pair of shoes."

So he said, "Whenever the meetin's over, boys, you'll come with me and I'll get y'all a pair of shoes."

So we went down to this mercantile store. We found out it was a clothin' store. We'd done learned a new word. We couldn't spell it, but we knowed what it was. We went in the store and he said, "I'm gonna give y'all a pair of shoes, but I don't want you to put your dirty feet in my clean shoes." So he gave us a pair of socks too and we put 'em on.

Well, you'll never guess what he brought out! I was so happy I didn't know what to do. It was a pair of them Red Rider tennis shoes that I wanted all my life! And he put them thangs on my feet and they fit perfect!!

I was so happy I didn't know what to do! Whew! I was so happy. He gave Byron a pair and said, "Y'all need a new shirt too." So he gave us both a red shirt.

Well, we was decked out! We was in high cotton! We had 204 dollars in our pocket in one-dollar bills. We had got a tombstone for our friend and we had a pair of them Red Rider tennis shoes. Them thangs cost 2 dollars. We could have bought us a pair but I didn't want to waste no money on no shoes. So we got it all.

Okahumpka

By Roland Lewis

Okahumpka – land between the great waters
Land where Chief Osceola and Billy Bowlegs flourished in God's creation
Fathers of the great Seminole Nation
Okahumpa – where Andy Jackson pursued the elusive Cree and Cherokee
into Chitty Chatty

I'm an Okahumpka man
As for me and my clan
We'll make our stand
On this Okahumpka sand

Okahumpka – where our great fathers made their stand
Land where springs clear and clean flow into Cypress and Bays, many to
this day unseen
Marshes and Oak Trees, Long Leaf Pines
Maples and Tupelo Gums through which the waters wind

I'm an Okahumpka man
As for me and my clan
We'll make our stand
On this Okahumpka sand

Riverboats ladened with stocks and barrels once graced your waves
But now are faint memory shadows in the sun's rays
Still the Wood Duck's squall and cranky Egret's call are heard among the
Cypress knees

I'm an Okahumpka man
As for me and my clan
We'll make our stand
On this Okahumpka sand

Sandhill Cranes and elusive Kites
Glide above the tree canopy
Unique to Florida alone
Their soaring is seen
Okahumpa-forever, Florida's Queen.

Album

Cast of Characters

Red Fussell – Author of this book. I've lived in Okahumpka, Florida all my life. The swamp and the big oak where the swing was is still there. That ole post office and railroad tracks is gone and the depot has been moved to Tampa to Florida Fair Grounds. All the orange trees is gone. The City of Leesburg owns the swamp, but I bet they don't know that log where we walked in to the island. The island in Lake Denham is gone. Not sure if the moonshine still is still there but Bugg Spring is still there. The Works house, where Byron lived, is gone and so is our house. The hotel burned in 1923. All 4 stores are gone. The current Highway 27 warn't built until around 1953. When I think of the swamp, it will always be there and will always be in my mind and heart.

Byron – My best friend growin' up. I put this book together for Byron. His health has been not all that good. We sit in the swing in his yard and talk about ole times. You probably noticed I don't spell well and my English isn't much better. But I'm not one who has a half-way friend. Byron and me have been friends for 'bout 80 years. When we was babies we bit each other. We fished, hunted, rode up and down the road, coon hunted, stole chickens, frog hunted. Just had a great time for many years.

Uncle Will – Yes, Uncle Will existed. He lived in Okahumpka and yes, I did love him. He was one of my best friends. I'll never forget the day Uncle Will cried when I left to go to the Army. When I come back he was the first one I saw.

When he died my brother and I paid for his funeral. He wore one of my dad's suits. Yes, he did like shine. And he did live in a log house in the swamp. My dad only whipped me 2 times in my life. One when I called Uncle Will an ole "black nigger". He whipped me with a plow line. Then made me cut Will's stove wood. The next time I found a bumble bee nest in the ground I plugged the hole with my foot and beat the ground with a stick. Out come a bumble bee through a crack and it stung Uncle Will over the eye. My dad got a switch and whipped my legs about 5 times. He knowed I wouldn't move my foot.

Evelyn – I have the most respect for Evelyn. When she went to the Okahumpka school she whupped about everybody in the school. If you crossed her, you got your nose rubbed in the clay.

But the thang that made me respect her was what she did with her life. Growin' up, her family lived in a barn with a dirt floor. They didn't have indoor plumbin', electricity or runnin' water. They slept in the hay loft outdoors. And they took a bath like we did, once a week. She didn't wear shoes, didn't have none My momma sewed her some clothes.

They moved to Leesburg and she finished high school and then went to Gainesville to college. She did odd jobs, anythin' she could and taught twelfth grade history. Just goes to show you that you can do anythin' if you want to.

Bill – Yes, Bill lived in Okahumpka. He would take an ole car and cut the body off and make a wooden body. Just about everyone in our town did fish, and Bill did take our boat. We let the air out of his tires a few times.

But he would take us to ballgames. He farmed some and drove a truck. He warn't a bad sort of a person, but he made the book more fun.

Glossary

Croker Sack—a sack of a rough material, like burlap

Hogback — Man-made berm-top road higher than the swamp water. Looks like the hog's back.

Holes & Knuckles — Marble game. If you lost a game of marbles your opponent got to shoot at your knuckles. It hurts.

Lighter Knot — Piece of pine tree full of sap. Burns very hot.

Model A Goat — Modified Model A car, sawed off to make a wooden bed to carry freight, also called a Hoover.

Okella — Ocala.

Kaolin — a soft, grayish clay used in making china.

Plaited — Braided.

Pole Cat — Skunk.

Rabbit Tobacco — A plant grown in the wild. A common tobacco substitute used by young boys in rural areas. When crushed the plant exudes a characteristic maple syrup scent.
Can be smoked for respiratory ailments or made into a relaxing tea. Has a mild sedative effect.

Red Bugs — Chiggers.

Sabal Palm: The sabal palm is the only palm native to Florida. The "heart of palm" is a soft area in the upper trunk of the palm. It is used in salads or as a cooked vegetable. The comon name for it is "swamp cabbage."

Sabal Palm in Florida.

A serving dish of swamp cabbage and steak

Shine or Swamp Water — Moonshine. Illegal home-made whiskey

Skeeters —Mosquitoes

Spanish Seed—Little black stick-like-lookin' seeds about the size of a safety pin, that stick to your clothes.

Stinging Nettle —Plant with fuzz on the leaves. Stings if brushed against. To get rid of the sting, you pee on it.

Red at fifteen or sixteen

Cracker Trivia

A true Florida Cracker, besides being born in Florida, is one who loves the land and nature. Loves growin' thangs in the soil, loves family and has deep sense of religion. But it also means putin' cracklin's in your bread dough and grits and makin' periwinkle soup and swamp cabbage and okra gumbo and ham hocks with collard greens and fried chicken in a cast iron skillet and puttin' homemade guava jelly in 'em cat-eye biskits.

When we was kids, we didn't have no tooth brush. I had my first tooth brush when I went to the Army. You had to have one there. Growin' up we brushed our teeth with a stem on the palmetto fan, flattened out with a hammer till it was soft. We used salt and bakin' soda. You never went to a dentist 'til you had a tooth ache.

Red in his twenties

We had groves of guava trees growin' when I was growin' up but they's all gone.

They's lotsa places with names that come from the Injuns. Yalaha is a little town goin' east on Hwy 48. Okahumpka is where I was born and raised and I still live there. They's a river named Palatlakaha, but if you grew up here you call it "Pe-ad'-a-lee-ka'-ha".

The Palatlakaha River

Near Bugg Spring

Epilogue

That's the end of this book. Someday I may write 'bout the later years and what we went through. But I would like to say a special thanks to Byron and his family for letting us use their names, and Patsy Ezell, for letting us use her name. Some of the names are fictitious and some of it is true. I would like to name all the names, but I couldn't do that.

I want to thank 2 more people. Had it not been for them, I could not have done this. That's Sandy Kruse and Ruth Williams. Bless their beat-beatin' hearts. I wrote out the book on paper, and they did the rest.

I got the idea for the book when I read *The Land Remembered* and all Patrick Smith's books. I saw my own self as I read them books.

They's so many people in this neighborhood that we shook up when we was kids. We loved 'em all. This old colored fella that we knowed, he really did exist. We didn't use his real name, but he did exist. And we worried the mess out of 'im. But we loved 'im too, jist like we did Uncle Will in the story.

The swamp is still over there. We did build a platform there. We did build a little ole house-like thang up in the trees. We did beat on that drum like we said we did. But we didn't make all that noise like we said. And we killed all them varmints, trapped all them quail, shot up 'em gators and skinned their britches offen 'em.

I hope you enjoyed this book. This is part of Byron's and my life.

God bless all them children.

Red

My best lifetime friend, Byron Works, passed away on April 6, 2016, just before this book went to print. I regret that Byron didn't have a chance to read "our" book. He would have enjoyed it because he did most of the things mentioned in the story.

Made in the USA
Columbia, SC
28 April 2021